Bobby.
You, like this book, are disgusting.
Love always,
Wallace

Pink Flamingos

and Other Filth

Three Screenplays by

JOHN WATERS

THUNDER'S MOUTH PRESS
NEW YORK

IN MEMORY OF DIVINE

PINK FLAMINGOS AND OTHER FILTH
Three Screenplays by John Waters

Published by
Thunder's Mouth Press
An Imprint of Avalon Publishing Group Inc.
245 West 17th St., 11th Floor
New York, NY 10011

AVALON
publishing group incorporated

Contents

Introduction to an Introduction 2005

An Introduction (2005) to an Introduction (1988)? A Gertrude Stein poem? An exercise in bait and switch? Yes, there's been a title change to the book—*Trash Trio* just didn't do it anymore. *Pink Flamingos* couldn't stand being a subtitle—it clawed its way right up to the top billing in "Books in Print."

Is there even one anecdote from *Pink Flamingos* that has not been fully exploited? Please! Don't make me tell the "eating shit" story again. Even if I discover the cure for cancer tomorrow and die the next day, the coprophasiastic ending of *Pink Flamingos* will run first in my obituary. The film has hardly mellowed in the can; the finale might seem even <u>worse</u> today. Now, there are laws against this kind of thing on film; then, there weren't. Would *Fear Factor* have pulled a similar stunt if we hadn't beaten the show to the punch?

When the twenty-fifth anniversary edition of *Pink Flamingos* was released on video, I was shocked that it climbed to number two on the Billboard chart. Number one was *Jerry McGuire* and number three was *The Rock*. In some . . . well, special supermarkets in West Hollywood, they even sold *Pink Flamingos* at the checkout counter right next to *TV Guide*. My favorite story was told by a friend who was watching *Anna Karenina* at the Angelika multiplex in New York. As the climactic love scene unfolded on film, you could hear Divine next door where *Pink Flamingos* was playing, bellowing the line: "Someone has sent me a bowel movement," ruining *Anna Karenina* for the entire audience.

3900 Greenmount Avenue, the Marbles' Baltimore home address in the film, and where I actually lived (with Mink Stole) at the time of the making of *Pink Flamingos*, is still there and from the outside looks almost exactly the same. I, decades later, met the owners of the house, proprietors of a high-end gourmet shop, and told them they ought to rent the *Pink Flamingos* video to see how their house looked when we lived there. "Oh, my God," the woman of the house later wailed, "Divine was licking my banister!" I didn't have the heart to tell her that the curse acted out in the film actually works. If there's someone you don't like, wait until they leave the room, quickly jump up and lick whatever piece of furniture they were sitting on (the more saliva the better), and after they come back in and sit back down something awful will happen to them. Try it. I'm not kidding.

Desperate Living is used to being the poor step-sister of *Pink Flamingos*. More popular now than when it first came out, *Desperate Living* still is the last of the old-school John Waters scream-a-thons. I see Liz Renay, the ex-gangster-moll star, a lot

JOHN WATERS AND LIZ RENAY TODAY.
(Photo from the collection of John Waters)

more these days, too. She lives in Las Vegas and seems to come to all my premieres much more than in the past. She even reunited with her *Desperate Living* on-screen lesbian girlfriend, Mole (Susan

Lowe), for the first time since we made the film at my New Museum show opening in New York. It was a thrill to see them together again after twenty-eight years. Liz looks great, too; "so happy she might explode" might be a good description of her senior-citizen glamour-girl image that she so carefully exaggerates. "What have you been up to?" I always ask and it seems Liz never stops working. "Oh, shooting another movie," she says batting her false eyelashes. "Which one?" I ask. "*Corpse Grinder II*," she giggles. "Where did you shoot that?" I ask impressed. "In my house," she replies nonchalantly. Liz Renay is actually the happiest person I know.

Jean Hill (Grizelda) is still around, too, and I was thrilled to have her back on screen in *A Dirty Shame*. She's a big girl with some health problems, so getting her up on the second floor fire escape for her scene was a logistical nightmare. Once in camera position, two assistants crouched right outside the shot, ready to catch her if she fell. But don't underestimate Miss Jean Hill, she was at the Baltimore premiere of *A Dirty Shame* in full regalia in a wheelchair. Even Kate Moss sat on her lap. "I'm a model, too," Jean said to her without a trace of irony.

How come no one has made a musical out of *Flamingos Forever*? I realize the chances of filming this sequel are slim: expensive to make, no stars would do it, guaranteed MPAA problems, and the death of midnight movies. But Broadway? Come on, it's got diva worship, muscle men, underwater ballet, journalist hostages, cute heroine-addicted children, joyful necrophilia, show-biz miracles, and flying turds. I mean, if this doesn't SING, what does? Come on, Marc Shaiman and Scott Wittman, you did such a great job with *Hairspray, the Musical*—can't you make this bird fly, too?

Introduction 1988

Finally, in the best Mickey Rooney–Judy Garland tradition, you can now put on my movies like little plays in the privacy of your own home. Some rainy Saturday afternoon, just call all your friends together and yell, "Hey, kids, let's do *Pink Flamingos!*" Every hideous word of these films is right here in black and white, so you don't have to rely on a vague memory of some midnight show you staggered into years ago in a questionable state of mind. In the light of day, on the printed page, these "celluloid atrocities" may seem even ruder than you remember. Say the dialogue out loud, even yell it like the characters do—you'll feel better. Do Divine's psychotic monologues and feel the tensions and distractions of everyday life melt away. You could even read along with the videos, getting the inflection just right, playing your favorite part in front of the mirror. Or, what the hell, play every single part yourself and watch your friends run from your house in a panic.

Here are my pre-"respectable" scripts, the ones the new *Hairspray* fans and all our parents would have a heart attack over if they read. These films are like my juvenile delinquents, and I'm proud of them. Very few mainstream critics supported this work; it was the fans—all you people with a dubious sense of humor—who made these movies a success. You've put up with a lot: bad prints, inconvenient show times in obscure, out-of-the-way theaters, even censored copies I had no control over. You've also been my ace in the hole with movie executives—they know you "open" my films (come out in droves the first weekend) with a bang. And I thank each and every one of you from the bottom of my black little heart!

Think of all the wonderful things you've bought me with royalties: a lifetime of cigarettes; books like *Autoerotic Fatalities, Sex and the Confessional, They Died in the Chair;* my gold lamé loafers that make people gag; my prize records, like "Annette's Scrapbook," "Connie Francis Sings Jewish Favorites," and "The Joey Heatherton Album"; even the collection of fake meat (bacon strips, hamburgers, steaks) that litters the tables of my home. You've helped me create a genre unto itself and I'm so happy I could easily start speaking in tongues.

Of course, these pages are populated with ghosts. David Lochary, Edith Massey, and my favorite actor in the world, Divine, are all gone now, but they're still in those film cans and videocassettes waiting to pop out at the drop of a hat. Without these actors and actresses, the films would have been nothing. Think of them when you read these pages, even say a little prayer—you're guaranteed some kind of fetishistic plenary indulgence.

Who would have ever thought eighteen years ago, while I was making an insane home movie with my friends in a field, that I'd still be talking about *Pink Flamingos* today? I'd certainly never imagined touring Japan with it, as I did a few years back, marveling at that country's censorship. Used to hassling over the "chicken fuck" and "dog shit" scenes with bluenoses everywhere, I was shocked to find these were okay. The only thing illegal was the showing of any pubic hair. Imagine my surprise at seeing the optical Japanese "bouncing ball" superimposed over every nude crotch in the film. Now the film was even dirtier and better than before.

Life imitates "art"? I hope not—for a while I needlessly worried over the similarities between a recent Philadelphia mass murderer and his "pit" of torture, and one of the most hideous scenes in *Pink Flamingos*, which it so closely resembled. Amazingly, someone seriously approached me about turning the film into an opera (still in the works). I never would have guessed that some scenes (the artificial insemination) would even offend *me* as I grew older. Who knows, this picture seems to have a life of its own—maybe one day, not too far off, we'll see *Pink Flamingos* on network TV.

And yes, for the thousandth, for the millionth, for the trillionth time, Divine really did eat dog shit at the end of the film. You've eaten shit too without realizing it: four years of college, ass-kissing jobs—we've all done it at one time or another in our lives. Divine was young, he was a trouper, and he was a professional—what more can I say? It was a touch of surrealism, maybe even a little magic in our young lives.

Almost nothing physical is left from that film. God hates mobile homes (that's why he sends tornadoes to them first), and even the carcass of the trailer we used as a setting has been hauled away by the new owners of the land. All that remains are the survivors of *Pink Flamingos*. Mary Vivian Pearce still works at the racetrack clocking horses for *The Racing Form*. She's a brunette now and nobody assumes she is Cotton in real life anymore. Still the only actress to have been in every one of my films, Mary Vivian can be spotted in *Hairspray* as the hairhopper mother with the giant red wig outside the studio on preteen day. Mink Stole, of course, still acts in my films and was last seen as the lead in *Sister Mary Ignatius* in Philadelphia. Cookie lives in New York, is now married, and has just finished her new book. Her son, who played Baby Noodles in *Pink Flamingos*, is now a teen-ager. Danny Mills (Crackers) is out on parole after being in jail for his involvement in "the largest LSD ring in America." Don't worry, Danny's in great shape, he even got a new front tooth. Channing, the Marbles' insane manservant, is a disc jockey in Provincetown, and Paul Swift, the demented Eggman, works in an antiques shop in Baltimore. And both the girls in the pit are just fine, thank you. Sue is married with two children and Linda is a psychologist in New York. Elizabeth, the gender-bender flasher in the park, lives with her husband, mother, and brothers in the same Philadelphia house she grew up in, and we get together every time I'm in town. Even the actor with the "singing asshole" is alive and well, working as a computer programmer in Baltimore. He claims he's "never once been recognized"—I guess the audience just wasn't concentrating on his face. He confides that his parents "still don't know" about his infamous role but when he tells people "they find it amusing. I lent the video to somebody at work, but she gave it back and didn't comment."

Desperate Living was the least successful of my films at the box office. I can't imagine why—a movie about a lesbian sex-change who realizes she made a mistake seems just what the doctor ordered for the mall cineplexes of Mid-America, but the general public didn't seem to agree. Some hard-core graduates of the "John Waters School" like it best of all, though, and in Europe they think it's political. In a few instances, the film was initially attacked by militant lesbians, but today the new breed of gay women come up to me and tell me how much they like it—which thrills me beyond belief since I always wished I *were* a lesbian (the literary kind who are usually so severe and smart). It's definitely my ugliest film, the least joyous and the loudest. Something to read if you're crashing from a glue high or contemplating suicide. Oh well, at least it has a happy ending.

There was a lot of new talent on board for *Desperate Living*. Besides the usual "Witches of Dreamland" (Mary Vivian, Cookie, Mink, Sharon, Marina), Susan Lowe had her first leading role as the monstrously butch Mole McHenry. Today, Susan is happily married with two children and continues her successful painting career while teaching art in an elementary school. She loves the film but was a bit mortified when a fellow teacher mentioned he had enjoyed her performance on video. Some of the other faculty and the students' parents might not give such good reviews. Liz Renay, the stripper–author–painter–personality–standup comedienne–movie star who played Muffy St. Jacques, now lives in Las Vegas and, although I've talked to her several times, I've never seen her since we made the film. I keep up with her exploits, though. I heard she was dating Frank Stallone, Sylvester's brother. Can't imagine what his mother had to say.

The biggest discovery, both literally and figuratively, was Miss Jean Hill, who played the killer maid Grizelda. At 5′1″ and 480 pounds (at last count), she is definitely a star to be reckoned with. In real life Jean is maybe the most outrageous woman I've ever met. She went on to become one of the top greeting-card models in the country. I loved it when strangers who weren't aware of her career but knew she had to be *somebody* asked what she did for a living and Jean blithely answered, "Model."

Flamingos Forever was the long-awaited (by nobody but me) sequel to *Pink Flamingos*. I never made the movie because nobody would give me the money. My first abortion; the only project I could never get off the ground. I spent two years trying, though, so I'm thrilled that it's included in this book. Even if it is "stillborn."

"Beyond the MPAA rating system," "nobody would pay to see it," and "atrocious" were a few of the producers' comments after reading the script. Maybe they were right. The whole movie seemed cursed from the beginning. In *Shock Value* I wrote, "I know I'll never make a sequel," which only goes to prove that I'm a liar. In hindsight, it probably *was* a bad idea, maybe even "career-icide." The exact opposite of "crossover" (that word has always been the bane of my existence). But for the budget I was asking ($600,000—insanity in itself), I'm still convinced the movie could have made money.

Even Divine wasn't crazy about doing it, although he agreed to make the film. The physical stunts (eating underwater, carrying Edith on his back in a baby pouch) made him nervous, as did the very mention of any scene with scatalogical overtones. The insurance companies would have surely balked at Jean Hill climbing around roofs and jumping down chimneys. The subject matter (male rape, necrophilia, child kidnapping, communism) didn't exactly make for a safe Hollywood pitch either. "Can't you have a hot young girl, maybe their long-lost cousin, come to live with Divine and family?" one hack producer asked. On the other hand, Edith, Mink, and Mary Vivian were ready and willing and I had all sorts of bizarre casting ideas in mind. Maybe even Danny could be coaxed back to the silver screen. Van Smith, the costume designer, and Vince Peranio, the art director, were prepared to really knock themselves out.

The first nail in the coffin of *Flamingos Forever* was Edith's death. There was not another actress in the world who could replace her. I finally gave up, even though Troma Films had agreed in principle to back it (their postproduction facilities made me nervous). Years later, right before we made *Hairspray,* a producer I had once approached did call to say he had the financing, but by now *Flamingos Forever* was dead and buried, at least on celluloid. But like Dracula from his grave, it's back on these pages. You can't keep a pretty girl down.

⸗ Pink ⸗
Flamingos

PINK FLAMINGOS
A Dreamland Production Written, Directed,
Filmed, and Edited by John Waters

Cast

Divine/Babs Johnson	DIVINE
Raymond Marble	DAVID LOCHARY
Cotton	MARY VIVIAN PEARCE
Connie Marble	MINK STOLE
Mama Edie	EDITH MASSEY
Crackers	DANNY MILLS
Channing	CHANNING WILROY
Cookie	COOKIE MUELLER
Eggman	PAUL SWIFT
1st Kidnapped Girl	SUSAN WALSH
2nd Kidnapped Girl	LINDA OLGEIRSON

Art Director   VINCENT PERANIO
Costumes and Makeup   VAN SMITH

Running Time: 95 minutes   Color

DIVINE, A.K.A. BABS JOHNSON

Long shot of pink-and-gray house trailer in the woods. It is dead of winter. A china kitten climbs the front of the trailer. A blue gazing ball, plaster chickens, and plastic pink flamingos decorate the lawn. The credits begin immediately—they are endless; every star and every extra is listed. The camera zooms in on the gazing ball and one of the flamingos. As credits end the atrocious voice of the Narrator begins. He has a thick Baltimore accent.

NARRATOR   Hello, moviegoers! This is Mr. J. speaking to you for Dreamland Studios. This beautiful mobile home you see before you is the current hideout of the notorious beauty Divine, the filthiest person alive.

Shot of Midnite *newspaper with photo of Divine on the cover. The headline reads "Exclusive! Photos of Divine— The Filthiest Person Alive."*

NARRATOR   Because of this cover story in one of your sleazier national tabloids, she has been forced to go underground, disguising her appearance and adopting the alias of Babs Johnson.

Camera returns to trailer exterior.

NARRATOR With her live her trusted traveling companion Cotton, her delinquent son Crackers, and her mentally ill mother Miss Edie. Let's take a peek inside.

The living room of the trailer. Miss Edie, a massive woman, sits in a child's playpen in a girdle and bra. Tacky 1950s furniture and cheesy leopard contact paper decorate the room. A small wall plaque reading "God Bless Our Mobile Home" is visible.

EDIE It's ten-thirty! Babs! Babs! Why isn't the eggman here? I'm starving to death for some eggs. Please, Babs, come in and give me my eggs.

Close-up of Babs' bare feet slipping into feather-trimmed gold slippers atop the zebra-patterned linoleum floor of her bedroom.

EDITH MASSEY AS MAMA EDIE, THE "EGG LADY"

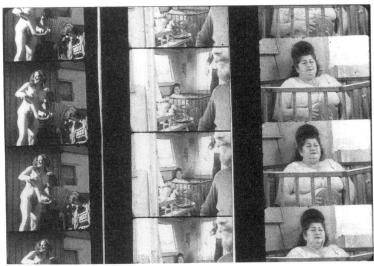

BABS   I'm coming, Mama, I'm coming. You can hold on.

Back to living room.

EDIE   Cotton! Cotton! Babs won't give me my eggs! Cotton, please come in here and give me my eggs.

Shot of Cotton lying on bed listening to 45 rpm records. She is very blond and pretty. Her wall is decorated with photos of musclemen.

COTTON   Be in in a minute, Edie, don't you worry. I'll fry you up some, honey.

Back to living room. Edie is getting panicked.

EDIE   EGGS! EGGS! EGGS!

EDIE, COTTON (MARY VIVIAN PEARCE), AND BABS
AT HOME IN THE TRAILER

Babs enters. She is quite fat and wears a yellow bouffant hairdo, shaved back to the middle of her head, garish make-up, and an ugly housedress.

BABS Good morning, Mama. I bet you're hungry.

EDIE Oh, Babs, I'm starving to death. Hasn't that eggman come yet? I love that eggman so much.

BABS *(As if speaking to a child)* No, he hasn't come yet, Mama, but we still have some eggs. I'll put some on for you. Did you sleep well?

EDIE Oh, Babs, I slept so well. Where did you get this train? Did you sleep in the caboose last night? How did you know I loved trains?

BABS Oh, it's not a train, Mama, it's our new mobile home and I sleep in the other room. We all have our own rooms this time; me, you, and Cotton. Crackers has that nice little shed right out back so he can have his friends in whenever he likes without waking us up. Isn't it wonderful? Now, you just sit tight and I'll fry you up some big grade-A treats. Over light today, Mama?

EDIE No, Babs, no. It's sunny out today. I want them sunny-side up. You know how I like them, Babs. You know how I like them.

BABS I know, Mama, I know. I'll be right back. *(She exits)*

As the Narrator's voice begins again, we see the exterior of a three-story row house. A sign with the address 3900 is on the small front lawn.

NARRATOR   Across town, located in the teeming metropolis known as downtown Baltimore, live Connie and Raymond Marble, two jealous perverts that hate Divine's fame and notoriety more than anything in the whole world. For Connie and Raymond Marble it was the beginning of the end!

Medium shot of Connie's office. She is interviewing a young woman. Connie sits regally behind her desk wearing a blue jeweled suit and rhinestone-trimmed cat-eye glasses. Her hair is the color of a red crayon.

CONNIE   Well, Miss Sandstone, after looking over your qualifications, my husband and I have decided that you are not exactly what we had in mind for the job. Not only have you never heard of Divine, which is one of the key elements in this particular job, you also seem to show a lack of general experience and, to be honest, we feel you to be sort of a dullard.

SANDY *(Taken aback)*   Well, why do you say that? I did everything you asked. I even found out who this Divine was.

CONNIE   Too late! Too late! Naturally you did everything I asked, my dear, or you would never have gotten to this plateau of the job placement test. I mean *surely* you can see our point—we're not in a position to just take anyone. This is a high-security job, as you can well imagine, and personally, we just don't feel you meet our . . . oh, how should I say? . . . our admittedly sometimes stringent screening process.

SANDY   Well, why did you hold me up for so long? Why did you keep asking me to come back? I had another job I could have taken. How could I get this information about Divine? I don't know her. You led me to believe I had this job.

CONNIE   Well, Miss Sandstone, Miss . . . *(She checks her records)* . . . Miss *Sandy* Sandstone, you just must have been wrong in your assumption, weren't you? I mean surely you've heard the expression "Don't count your chickens." Well, APPLY IT! I never gave you an answer on this whole thing, and as far as you believing that you had the job, well, I've never even considered that you would be the applicant we would choose. You don't know enough. I mean, I wish everyone was like you and had never heard of Divine but, unfortunately, it just isn't like that. Now if you wouldn't mind, I do have a busy day ahead of me; there's really nothing left to discuss.

SANDY   What am I supposed to do now? That's what I'd like to know.

CONNIE   You can eat shit for all I care, Miss Sandstone, or eat anything that you like or do anything that you like, just don't assume that *I* want to know your troubles. Now, if you wouldn't mind, I'm a busy woman with a full day's work ahead of me. Please remove yourself from my office!

SANDY *(Jumping up)*   You're a real cunt, do you know that? A real fucking cunt! How can you be so shitty to people? How can you stand yourself?

CONNIE   I guess there's just two kinds of people, Miss Sandstone: my kind of people and assholes. It's rather obvious which category you fit into. Have a nice day.

SANDY   Eat the bird, bitch! *(She exits)*

Out back of Babs' trailer, we see her son Crackers' shed. It is crudely made out of scrap wood and is decorated with hubcaps. Crackers stands in front of it holding a live chicken. He is dressed in Levi's and an old shirt, has long hair, and one of his front teeth is missing.

CRACKERS   You ready, Ma? You ready yet?

Babs appears on back porch of trailer and yells.

BABS   I'm ready, darling, just let me say good-bye to Mama and Cotton. I'll be out in a minute, honey.

CRACKERS   Okay, Ma, but get the lead out of your ass or I'll be late for my date.

BABS   All right.

CRACKERS *(Begins petting chicken and talking to it)*   Yes, won't I be late for my date? You all are going to love my date. I'm going to bring her back real soon for you all to enjoy.

Cotton sits in the living room of the trailer next to Edie in her playpen.

EDIE   What do you mean "Humpty Dumpty was an egg"? How could a person be an egg, Cotton, how could a person be an egg?

CRACKERS (DANNY MILLS)

PINK FLAMINGOS

COTTON (*Patiently*) Well, he had little arms and little legs and he could walk and talk and all just like he was a person, only he was an egg, a little egg all dressed up.

EDIE (*Laughs hysterically*) Tell it to me again, Cotton.

COTTON You should be learning it by now, Edie. Now listen carefully. "Humpty Dumpty sat on a wall. / Humpty Dumpty had a great fall. / All the king's horses and all the king's men / Couldn't put Humpty together again."

EDIE Hahahahaha! (*She laughs uncontrollably, wildly shaking the bars to her playpen*)

COTTON Do you get it, Edie? Do you understand?

EDIE Tell me some more egg stories, Cotton, please tell me some more stories.

Babs enters in gold-print skintight dress, gold Spring-o-laters, fox wrap, and another layer of heavy makeup. She looks staggeringly bizarre.

BABS I'm on my way.

COTTON You sure are dressed up, Babs, you look real pretty.

BABS (*Sits down on a tacky couch*) Oh, thank you, Cotton. A girl can never tell who she might run into when she's downtown. Why, I'm all dressed up and ready to fall in love.

COTTON I kinda wish I was going out too, but I think Crackers is bringing his lady friend out here and I don't want to miss that—it's usually a pretty good show.

BABS   Oh, I know. You can go into town next time I go, it's just those errands I have to run. Besides, you and Crackers will have a pretty good time right here; that little shed's just perfect!

COTTON   I know it, Babs. It will be the first time we've had anyone out here and I can't wait to see how it works. I hope *she* doesn't give us any trouble.

BABS   Oh, I wouldn't worry about that. Crackers has a pretty good eye for what he likes. Just say a little prayer *I* find a little something. Why, I haven't fallen in love in three whole days and I'm just ITCHING to find somebody with a little imagination.

EDIE *(Blurting)*   BYE-BYE BABS, BYE-BYE BABS. BYE-BYE BABS! BYE-BYE BABS!

BABS *(Visibly annoyed)*   Mother, you do not have to raise your voice and you don't have to yell. We're all right here. We can all hear you!

EDIE *(Crying)*   I do have to yell. I'm starving to death and that eggman ain't gonna come and I know it.

BABS   You know he never comes till later, Mother.

COTTON *(Comforting Edie, hugging her)*   She'll be all right. Go on, Babs. *(To Edie)* You want some hard-boiled eggs to nibble on while you're waiting?

EDIE *(Sobbing)*   Yes, yes.

COTTON   I bet you do.

Babs shakes her head in disbelief and exits out front door.

COTTON Bye, Babs, and don't forget the party food.

BABS Okay.

Babs walks out front door of trailer and onto the lawn.

BABS Crackers, I'm ready!

Crackers approaches, ready to leave for the city. He has a sheathed knife strapped to his belt.

CRACKERS Let's go, Mama. I'm late for my date.

BABS Oh, but honey, how will you ever get back from downtown?

CRACKERS We'll hitch, probably, Ma. It ain't hard. You can let me off at the Etta Gown Shop. That's where I'm supposed to meet the little lady. I just hope she's ready for a little action.

BABS Oh, honey, I know what you mean. I wouldn't mind finding a little action myself. But then you shouldn't have much trouble with your date, that is if she has anything on the ball. Just hope she likes to experiment. You know what I mean, a little sweet-talkin' goes a long, long way. Give me your hand, honey.

Babs and Crackers walk down wooded path, holding hands. Their garish appearance clashes with the idyllic country setting.

Shot of white 1961 Cadillac.

DIVINE STEPS OUT

PINK FLAMINGOS

They get in car and pull off.

Shot of power window going down.

Close-up of Coup de Ville insignia.

They drive along country road and purposely try to run over a jogger. Narrowly missing being hit, the startled jogger flees into the woods.

Close-up of Babs laughing.

A cloddish soldier is seen hitchhiking. They stop the Cadillac to give him a ride but as he runs to the car they pull off. Crackers gives him the finger.

The soldier shakes his fist as car vanishes, and he accidentally falls in a ditch.

Babs again laughs hysterically.

They park on city street, kiss good-bye, and go their separate ways.

We see Babs walk down a block with huge red graffiti on the wall behind her: "Free Tex Watson."

Connie Marble's office later in the day. She appears to be in a nasty mood. Impatiently she sounds her desk buzzer, which can be heard all over the house.

CONNIE   Channing! Channing!

Living room of Marbles' home. Channing, their butler, sits on a couch surrounded by movie posters and religious statues, reading a National Enquirer *with the headline "The People Around You Can Make You Sick." He has medium-long hair and wears a servant's pink uniform.*

CHANNING *(Hearing the buzzer)* Jesus Christ! *(He throws the paper down and walks offscreen)*

Channing enters Mrs. Marble's office.

CONNIE   Are they here yet?

CHANNING   They've been waiting.

CONNIE   WELL, SHOW THEM IN!

Channing returns to living room. Two women, Etta and Merle, are nervously waiting. Etta has an extremely high white bubble hairdo and wears a silver lamé dress. Merle has short hair and is dressed very masculinely.

CHANNING   Mrs. Marble will see you now.

ETTA *(Jumps up)*   Come on, Merle, she's ready to see us.

MERLE   I'm comin', I'm comin'.

They all enter Connie Marble's office.

CONNIE   Hello.

ETTA *(Nervously)*   Hello, Mrs. Marble. We've been so excited about this all week, me and Merle, well, we can hardly sleep at night just waiting to see little Noodles' face.

MERLE   And, shit, we usually sleep pretty good. Me and Etta are gonna have to really settle down once we get Noodles home. It's gonna be a lot different with a baby around.

CONNIE   Yes, well, as I said, Mr. Marble and I are about ninety percent certain that you will get Noodles, but first, have a seat, so I can briefly recheck your application.

Cut to the dungeonlike cellar of the Marbles' home. The floor is covered with old lumber and rocks. The rotting corpse of a young woman is visible and a newborn baby lies nearby. Another woman, Suzie, is chained to the floor and is eating out of a dog's plastic bowl. She wears a torn nightgown, black 1930s heels, and has sores all over her face. Her hair is matted and filthy and she is about five or six months pregnant. Channing climbs down ladder into the torture pit.

CHANNING   Don't say anything, all right? Just don't say a word.

SUZIE   *(Jumping up from her dinner and pointing to corpse)*   When are you gonna get her out of here?!

CHANNING *(Picking up baby))*   Come on, little Noodles, you just found a new home.

SUZIE   Oh, that's real nice! Poor fucking Alice dies giving birth and you can't even bother to move the body. And now that bitch has sold the kid! Poor baby. And you, you suckling, can't even get me my tranquilizers. You shithead, where are my pills?! That bitch can afford it—she's got another couple of grand coming for this one—can't she at least give me my fucking pills?

CHANNING   I said don't talk to me when I come down here.

SUZIE I don't give a fuck what you said, you fucking pig. Get this body out of here, it's making me sick! When are they gonna get another one? What poor girl will they get next? I know they'll get another one. Just like when I came here, I replaced somebody, didn't I? You fucking little dingleberry. That's what you're like, you fucking ball of shit!

CHANNING I said SHUT UP! Just shut up and don't talk to me when I come down here.

Back to Connie's office. Channing enters with the baby. Etta and Merle both jump up oohing and aahing, trying to hold the baby.

ETTA Oh, look how pretty she is.

CHANNING *(Refusing to hand over the baby)* Wait a minute. Connie, do they get this?

CONNIE *(Smiling)* Yes they do, Chan.

ETTA Look how pretty she is. *(Holding the baby)* Oh, Merle, I'm so happy.

MERLE And baby, if you're happy, I'm happy. That's what I'm living for; you, me, and now, little Noodles.

ETTA Thank you, Mrs. Marble. Without you we could never have been this happy. You are a wonderful, wonderful person.

CONNIE Thank you, ladies. If it wasn't for you I wouldn't be in this business and that's all I care about is satisfying my customers and making sure the babies are placed in good homes.

MERLE & ETTA   Thank you.

CONNIE   Bye-bye, now.

Babs struts down a crowded Baltimore street, swinging her hips and flashing a smile. The camera is hidden in a moving car, so the mostly black crowd of downtown shoppers reacts with astonishment, laughing, pointing, and, in some cases, jumping back in fright. Everyone else is warmly dressed for winter. Babs wears only her sleeveless, gold-printed cocktail dress and spike heels.

Babs enters a small grocery store. Other shoppers can be seen selecting bread, etc. After looking over a canned-goods display, she approaches the butcher and orders a steak. He picks one, wraps it, and hands it to her. Babs carefully surveys the store for detectives, unwraps the steak, and sticks it up her dress and into her crotch. A look of bliss comes over her face when she feels the cold steak against her warm flesh. Just as she is leaving the store, a crazed hippie approaches her squeezing a pack of hot dogs and panting. Appalled, Babs exits the store as the hot-dog pervert falls to his knees, his tongue hanging out, moaning.

Shot of Babs' spike heels climbing the steps of a Baltimore park.

She takes a walk around the park, pausing to gaze at the Baltimore skyline.

Camera follows Babs as she descends park steps. A giant American flag blows in the wind behind her.

Continuing her walk, Babs is seen in front of the mansions in a rich part of the city. She casually strolls up to one of the estates' plush grounds and urinates, wiping herself with a tissue from her handbag and throwing the soiled Kleenex to the ground. She slowly walks away, defiantly swinging her hips.

Connie Marble's office. We see Connie reading the Midnite *with Divine on the cover and the "Filthiest Person Alive" headline. Connie is fuming, jumps up, and rips the paper in shreds.*

CONNIE   We'll *see* who's the filthiest person alive! We'll just see! And where is that Raymond? Where is he? How could he leave me alone when there's so much to be taken care of?! *(Sobbing)* Oh, please come home, Raymond. I need you so badly.

Exterior of Maryland Employment Service. Two female secretaries walk by on the way to their lunch break. Raymond Marble's head suddenly pops up from behind a wall. He has bright blue hair and wears a white sports jacket. It is obvious that Raymond is completely engrossed in spying on the two secretaries.

The secretaries walk into a public park, sit down, and begin to eat their lunch.

Close-up of Raymond Marble watching them through binoculars. He slowly sneaks up on them, all the while lightly groping himself.

The two young women continue to eat and chat.

Raymond is suddenly right behind them wearing a ridiculously theatrical face mask. He pulls open his coat and flashes his penis at them. His pubic hair is blue and a foot-long hot dog is tied to the end of his member.

The secretaries recoil in horror and run away, forgetting their purses.

Raymond chuckles, picks up the forgotten purses, and runs away laughing.

Raymond drives his black 1959 Cadillac limousine to a parking space in front of his house.

Close-ups of the tail fins, rear lights, and Cadillac insignia.

Raymond gets out of car, dusts himself off with a whisk broom, and enters his home.

Shot of a young woman named Cookie riding in backseat of a cab. She wears a red coat and a black fancy hat.

COOKIE   Can't you hurry, driver? I'll be late for my appointment.

DRIVER   Going as fast as I can without breaking the law, lady. 3900 Greenmount, right?

COOKIE *(Rudely)*   That's what I said, wasn't it?

The cab stops.

DRIVER $2.30.

PINK FLAMINGOS

COOKIE *(Jumping out of cab)*   You can shove $2.30, hack!

Driver jumps out and chases her, yelling and cursing.

Cookie has just entered the Marbles' living room. Raymond helps her off with her coat and they sit as Connie enters with a tray of sandwiches.

CONNIE   Well, hello, Cookie. I do hope you're hungry.

COOKIE *(Taking a sandwich)*   I could go for a sandwich. Mmm—baloney. Well . . . I'll get right to the point. I can get you information about Divine, lots of information I think, if things go well today. I have a date with her son Crackers.

RAYMOND   This is, of course, an encouraging development.

CONNIE   This is an important assignment, Cookie. We could all benefit—you financially, and Raymond and I, well, our social standing is involved to a great degree.

Close-up of framed photo of Manson family member Susan Atkins on the table.

COOKIE   I may have to degrade myself in front of Divine's son. He's into a very strange sex scene. I may have to put up with unheard-of atrocities in order to pump the information you need out of him. But first I have to know exactly what you need to know, because my so-called date is this afternoon.

RAYMOND   Cookie, as you know, Divine has achieved a sort of fame lately, both locally and on the national level. You may have heard the term "the filthiest person alive"?

COOKIE   I have heard the term, yes. The papers call her that and she is known as that to a limited extent in your more crime-conscious sections of the city.

CONNIE   We feel this to be an untrue statement. We feel Raymond and I far surpass her in every aspect of the term "filth." As you know, we run a baby ring. Oh, it's really a very simple process. We keep two girls at all times who are impregnated by Channing, our rather fertile servant. We sell the babies to lesbian couples and then we invest the money in various businesses around town.

RAYMOND   We own a few pornography shops plus we front money to a chain of heroin pushers in the inner-city elementary schools.

CONNIE   We feel the attention that's been focused on Divine is most unfair. She is merely a common thief and murderer. Unfortunately for us, our line of work limits our chances for publicity and travel but this does not mean we wish to go unnoticed! After all, we've not worked all these years in order to be upstaged by this fat hog that calls herself Divine.

RAYMOND   So we must catch her off guard, you see, before she realizes she is being attacked. We need information as to how they live, where they live, how many people, their names, their daily schedules for the week. In other words, we want to know how we can plague her the most, how we can make her life as miserable as possible, how we can prove to her that she is shit compared to us, shit compared to the filth we have in our minds, shit compared to what we know to be the filthiest life.

Long frontal shot of the trailer.

NARRATOR   Little does Crackers know that his so-called date is really a spy sent by the Marbles.

Crackers and Cookie enter the trailer living room. Edie is asleep in her playpen, snoring loudly. Egg leavings cover her face and chest, and a bowl of half-eaten eggs sits by her feet.

CRACKERS   This is my grandma, Edie.

COOKIE   What's . . . what's the matter with her?

CRACKERS   What's the matter with her? There ain't nothing the matter with her, she's just my grandma, that's all.

COOKIE   Why are those eggs all over her face?

CRACKERS   I guess she was just hungry, that's all. See, she sort of has some problems. Nothing serious, but you know, she just loves eggs, always has. Sit tight, I'll go see if Miss Cotton's up yet.

As Crackers exits, Cookie starts snooping around the living room looking for information.

Cotton's bedroom. She sits on the bed in a nervous state, frantically puffing on a cigarette. Crackers rushes in.

CRACKERS   She's here, Miss Cotton, she's here! Shouldn't be long now before I get it going, that is, if she cooperates and SHE WILL.

COTTON   Oh, Crackers, I'm so excited. I've just been sittin' right here ever since you left. What's she like? Does she have a nice body? What are you gonna do for me today, honey? Something I haven't seen, I hope.

CRACKERS   Miss Cotton, I got something in mind today I never ever tried before; something very exciting for me. My little chickens are going to be in the show today, Cotton. Me and some nice juicy plump chickens.

COTTON *(Getting more and more aroused)*   I need this so bad, Crackers. Make it better than you did last time!

CRACKERS   What was the matter with that one? You said you liked that show.

COTTON   Oh, I did, I did! It was just that you were so fucking beautiful in that one, that now I want more! I gotta see more, Crackers, more than I've already seen. Could we have some blood in this one? Just a little bit? And take off your clothes slower, and don't let HER ruin it!

CRACKERS   Miss Cotton, you're gonna dig this one. It's gonna be better than anything I ever did before. I can feel it in my blood, all through my body. You know I only do it for you. It's only you watching me that gets me off, you know that. I'll make it special today, I promise. *(He attempts to caress her)*

COTTON *(Panicked)*   Please be careful not to touch me!

CRACKERS *(Jumping back)*   I ain't touching you! I ain't touching you!

Trailer living room. Cookie is still looking around as Edie wakes up.

EDIE   Oh . . . hi, pretty little face. Pretty little face you've got there.

COOKIE   Oh . . . hello . . . I'm Cookie, I understand you're Edie, Crackers' grandmother.

EDIE *(Cackles)*   Edie, Schmedie, Hedie! Hahaha! Is Babs back from shopping for the birthday party? I'm gonna go; I got a party dress.

COOKIE *(All ears)*   When is the party?

EDIE   Oh, Babs' birthday. Are you the eggman?

COOKIE   No . . . no . . . I'm not. Where's Crackers' mother?

EDIE   She's calling all the people to invite them to the party and *I'm* gonna go.

Crackers enters with Cotton.

CRACKERS   I see you're up, Granny. *(Edie cackles) (To Cotton)* This is Miss Cotton, she's one of my roommates.

COOKIE *(Extends her hand as if to be kissed)*   Charmed, I'm sure.

COTTON *(Ignoring it)*   Hello, Cookie. You sure are a fine-looking young woman. Crackers has told me about you. *(To Crackers)* Why don't you show her the shed? *(To Cookie)* You'll like it out there, it's so private.

COOKIE   I'd love to see it.

CRACKERS   C'mon, Cookie, I'll go show you my chickens.

COOKIE You have chickens? I love little chickies!

Crackers and Cookie exit. Cotton rushes from window to window watching them as they approach Crackers' shed.

Cotton sneaks across yard to back of shed, where she watches the couple through a screen window.

The interior of the shed. Completely bare except for a torn mattress and a few live chickens wandering about. Crackers is already naked as he roughly undresses Cookie. As they begin to make love, Cookie's face begins to show horror as she realizes Crackers is stuffing live chickens between their bodies.

Cotton watches through rear window in a state of obvious sexual excitement.

COOKIE (COOKIE MUELLER), COTTON, AND CRACKERS
PREPARE FOR AN ODD SEXUAL ENCOUNTER

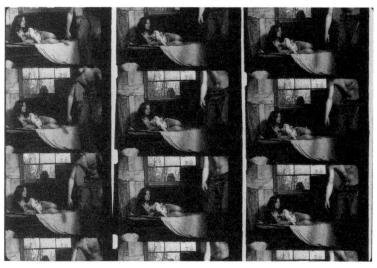

Crackers becomes wilder, forcing the startled chickens between Cookie's legs. Cookie begins screaming.

COOKIE No! Christ, no!

CRACKERS *(Struggling)* Hold 'em!

COOKIE *(Pushing away chickens)* No! God! No! No!

CRACKERS Hold it! Hold these goddamn chickens!

COOKIE Chickens! God, all these chickens! These fucking things hurt. *(Moaning and screaming)* God, you're crazy.

Crackers slits a chicken's throat and stuffs the bloody chicken between Cookie's legs and then throws himself wildly on top of her. Blood is everywhere and Crackers is wild with passion.

THE "CHICKEN FUCK"

Cotton is panting, still watching through window. At the sight of the blood, she faints from passion.

Cut to back lawn of trailer. The Eggman, dressed entirely in white, enters from trailer rear. He is carrying a suitcase.

EGGMAN   Eggman! Eggman! Anybody home?!

The living room of the trailer. Edie is still in her playpen and goes wild when she hears the Eggman's voice.

EDIE   Cotton! Cotton! I'm in here! I hear the Eggman! In here! In here, Mr. Eggman! Eggs! Eggs! Oh, help! God! God! In here! In here, Mr. Eggman! Here I am! The Eggman! The Eggman!

The Eggman and Cotton enter. The Eggman sits next to Edie's playpen and Cotton sits in a hideous easy chair.

EGGMAN   Hello, li'l Edie! How's my little princess today?

EDIE *(Blushing)*   Oh, Mr. Eggman.

COTTON   Mr. Eggman, we're having a party for Babs on Thursday and we'd like you to come as Edie's date.

EGGMAN   Well, I would be honored to attend, especially with such a beautiful date.

He opens his suitcase. Inside are dozens of eggs, mounted for display.

EGGMAN   And now, Edie, what will it be today? I have grade-A extra large, I have grade-A large, I have medium, I have small. I have brown, I have white. Why, just look at these. *(He holds up some eggs for Edie to inspect)* So fresh you could barely believe it. Why, they're just begging to be scrambled or fried or poached or hard-boiled or all-around ready to be thrown into a big fat juicy omelet. How about it, Edie? What'll it be for the lady the eggs like the most?

EDIE *(Beside herself with joy)*   I want them all! I'll have the brown ones, those great big white ones, and I'll have those over there and I want some for frying and for scrambling, and, oh, God, those over there . . .

COTTON   All right, Edie, we'll buy them all for you. How about that?

EDIE   Oh, Cotton, you make me so happy; you and the eggman. Please, Mr. Eggman, don't ever quit your job! I always want eggs, always and always and always.

MAMA EDIE AND THE EGGMAN (PAUL SWIFT)

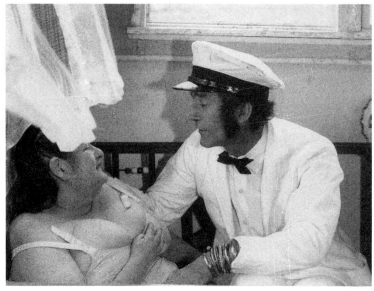

EGGMAN   Miss Edie, as long as there are chickens layin' and trucks drivin' and my feet walkin', you can be sure I'll bring you the finest of the fine, the largest of the large, and the whitest of the white. In other words, that thin-shelled ovum of the domestic fowl will never be safe as long as there are chickens layin' and I'm alive, because I AM YOUR EGGMAN AND THERE AIN'T A BETTER ONE IN TOWN!

EDIE *(Overcome with love)*   Oh, Mr. Eggman.

Connie and Raymond Marble are seated in the backseat of their Cadillac limousine. Channing is chauffeuring them as they cruise the neighborhoods in search of young women to kidnap.

CONNIE   Nothing but these fucking jerk-off hippies on the road today. Oh, where are their little pig girl friends? God, I get so tired of just driving around, driving around.

CHANNING *(Offscreen)*   Here's one up ahead.

CONNIE   Pull over!

RAYMOND *(Looking out window)*   M-m-m-m-m, she looks real good.

CONNIE   She'll do just fine.

A pretty young hitchhiker, Linda, gets in the car. She sits in the backseat between the Marbles.

LINDA   Thanks. Wow, where did you get this beautiful car?

RAYMOND *(Rudely)*   At a car dealer, where did you think?

CONNIE   Where are you going?

LINDA   Just downtown. Anywhere near Howard Street.

CONNIE   Oh? . . . Meeting someone?

LINDA   Yeah.

CONNIE   WHO?!

LINDA *(Beginning to get nervous)*   My boyfriend and a couple of other guys. Why?

RAYMOND   Going to a gang bang or something?

LINDA *(Shocked)*   What? Hey, what's with you two?

CONNIE *(Grabbing her)*   We just wondered where you were planning to spread your VD today, that's all, hussy!

LINDA   Hey, I don't think that's necessary.

CONNIE   Oh you don't, huh? Well, how'd you like to fuck my chauffeur? He's got a real horse dick on him.

LINDA *(Scared)*   Come on, just let me out here. This is fine.

RAYMOND   Why do you want to get out here? This isn't downtown.

CONNIE *(Shrieking)*   We're nowhere near Howard Street! What's the matter? You afraid it ain't big enough for you?

LINDA *(Struggling to jump out)*   Cut it out! Just let me out here!

CONNIE *(Shoving her)*   Sit back! *(To Channing)* Give me the rag!

LINDA   Get the fuck off of me! Please.

Connie takes a cloth soaked in chloroform and forces it to Linda's mouth. She quickly passes out.

RAYMOND *(Pleased)*   There, she's out now.

The torture pit. Suzie is still chained, squatting and crying. Channing enters carrying Linda, who is still unconscious.

CHANNING   I have a new friend for you.

SUZIE   Already? You got one already? Is she asleep or is she dead? Did you just kill her? Where'd they get this one?

CHANNING *(Chaining Linda to the floor)*   Hitchhiking, just like you were. Doesn't pay to hitchhike these days, does it?

SUZIE   And I guess you're gonna fuck her now, is that it? Right in front of me? The poor girl that has to fuck you! Thank God, I don't remember it! Thank God, you spared me at least that.

CHANNING   I have a surprise for you this time. I don't even have to touch her.

SUZIE How did you get out of that part of the job? Did your boss finally decide someone else would do it? Who? Her slimy boyfriend? Is she going to let that fag do it right in front of me? That whore!

CHANNING Oh, no, this is a surprise for Connie and Raymond too. I have it all figured out this time. I don't even have to touch her.

SUZIE Why did you have to touch me? How could I have a child by you? What a repulsive thought!

Channing pulls down his pants to his knees and begins to masturbate. His back faces the camera. Suzie is appalled.

SUZIE Oh, you pig! You animal! Oh, my God! Right in front of me! Stop it, you asshole! How vile can you be?

CHANNING *(Trying to concentrate)* Shut up! You'll see, just shut up!

SUZIE I swear I'm going to throw up on you, Chan. I swear I'm gonna puke if you don't stop it!

CHANNING *(Wildly)* Turn your head if it makes you sick! Don't watch. Think of how sick it made me to touch you and now . . . this one!

Channing moans in orgasm.

Suzie vomits all over herself.

Close-up of Channing sucking semen from his palm into hypodermic syringe and then performing artificial insemination on Linda.

SUZIE YOU REPULSIVE PIG! YOU HATE HER SO MUCH YOU'D GET HER PREGNANT THIS WAY!? STOP IT, YOU FILTHY ANIMAL!!

Connie and Raymond's bedroom. They are both wildly involved in a rather bizarre sexual act. Connie has her hair done like a man's and wears men's Jockey underpants. Raymond has his hair done in a woman's bouffant up-sweep and wears blue lace panties. As the scene begins, they are in sixty-nine position sucking each other's feet passionately.

The phone rings.

RAYMOND Shit, I'll get it.

CONNIE *(Sucking his toes)* Just let me finish you off!

RAYMOND It might be Cookie.

Phone rings again.

CONNIE Come on, you're almost there.

RAYMOND *(Reluctantly pulling away from her feet)* It's probably Cookie with the information.

CONNIE Answer it, then! Answer it!

RAYMOND *(Picking up receiver)* Marbles' residence.

Cookie is in her mother's Early American kitchen. During the entire phone conversation the camera jumps back and forth between Cookie's kitchen and the Marbles' bed-room.

COOKIE   Mr. Marble, this is Cookie. . . . No. . . . No. . . . I'm all right. I'm back at my mother's. I was afraid to come directly there, I thought maybe they'd be following me. Look, I have to have my money immediately.

RAYMOND   Of course you'll get your stool-pigeon money. Why on earth are you so suspicious?

COOKIE   Naturally, I'm going to question you about the money. You have no idea of what I went through today, and you *DID* call yourself the "filthiest people alive." What kind of credit rating is that?

RAYMOND   We need that information immediately so we can prepare our little surprise for that slut! Hold on a minute. *(To Connie)* She's afraid we won't pay her.

CONNIE   Let *me* talk to her. *(She grabs phone from Ray-mond)* Cookie, this is MRS. Marble. What's this nonsense about the money? Of course we will pay you.

COOKIE   Look, I'll tell you everything but you have to meet me right away with the money—all two thousand dollars of it in twenty-dollar bills.

CONNIE   We'll meet you at Harry Little's Sub-Shop on Twenty-fifth Street. You name the time.

RAYMOND   *(Grabbing the phone back)*   All right, now give us the information immediately. How do we even know you were there?

COOKIE   Oh, I was there all right, Mr. Marble. Divine is living under the name of Babs Johnson.

RAYMOND   Babs Johnson.

CONNIE   Babs Johnson?! Oh, what a stupid fucking name! Sounds like a chimpanzee on a tire swing.

RAYMOND   She's living in a trailer in Phoenix, Maryland.

CONNIE *(Grabs receiver)*   Who does she live with? ... Her mother? She lives with her mother and her mother sleeps in a playpen!

RAYMOND   Like a baby? Oh, God, how heartwarming.

CONNIE   ... And her son ... and her traveling companion. ... *Birthday?* ... A party? When?! ... Oh, how perfect! That pig will never get away with it. Never! Never! Never! It will be her most embarrassing birthday yet!

COOKIE   I should be there in about twenty minutes. You better be there or I'll tell Crackers everything about you, too!

CONNIE   Thank you, Cookie. *(She hangs up)* At last our plan can begin! Are you ready for phase one, Raymond? Oh God, at last we can show her, at last we can put our plan into effect. I only wish I could see her face, her fat little face, when she realizes that there is indeed someone filthier. She can EAT the cover of *Midnite,* she can eat all of her publicity in front of her rotten little party guests. Is her present ready?

RAYMOND *(He gets a small gift-wrapped package)*   I've had it for months, Connie. All ready. Special delivery. Phase one: the filthiest gesture in the world. Her little surprise package. For over a year now, this has been only a dream, only a prayer, but we have her address now! Oh, Connie, at last the Battle of Filth shall begin.

They both dive for each other's feet and begin sucking.

CONNIE   Oh, I love you, Raymond! I love you more than anything in the whole world. I love you even more than my own filthiness, more than my hair color. Oh God, I love you more than the sound of bones breaking, the sound of the death rattle, even more than my own shit do I love you, Raymond.

RAYMOND   And I, Connie, also love you more than anything I could imagine—more than *my* hair color, more than the sounds of babies crying, dogs dying, even more than the thought of original sin itself. I am yours, Connie, eternally united to you through an invisible cord of finely woven filth that even God Himself could never ever break.

Connie and Raymond are seen entering a local branch of the post office.

Interior post office. Quick shot of Nixon's portrait. They take package wrapped in brown paper to mailing window. A post office employee stamps the package "Special Delivery" and we see it is addressed to "Babs Johnson, a trailer, Phoenix, Maryland." The return address is "The Filthiest People Alive."

Exterior of trailer. Babs is frying the steaks she shoplifted on a grill on the front lawn. She hums show tunes and wears tight black slacks and a fake leopard halter top.

Interior of trailer. Edie is in her playpen still dressed in girdle and bra. Babs enters with the steaks.

BABS *(Looking toward Cotton's bedroom)* Cotton! Dinner's on! *(She rings a cowbell and yells out the window)* Crackers, dinner's ready!

Shot of Crackers, lying nude on his bed, surrounded by chicken corpses.

Back inside trailer. Babs is seated next to Edie's playpen.

BABS Well, you're looking pretty chipper, Mama. How was that Eggman today?

EDIE Oh, Babs, he's gonna come to the party as my date, and Cotton bought me so many eggs today. Look at these! *(She holds up bowl of eggs)* So many little eggies and I'm still starvee and I'm gonna eat them all before I go to sleepee. *(Laughs)*

Enter Cotton in full skirt, black jeweled leotard top, and cowboy boots.

COTTON Mmmm—smells delicious, Babs.

BABS *(Serving steak)* Thank you, Cotton. It should, I warmed it up when I was downtown today in my own little oven.

EDIE Babs, where do eggs come from?

BABS   From little chickens, Mama. They lay them and we eat them.

EDIE   But suppose someday there weren't any chickens. Would that mean there wouldn't be any eggs?

BABS   I don't think you have to worry about that, Mama.

EDIE   But . . . but it is true, Babs? If there weren't any chickens, there wouldn't be any eggs? Is that true?

BABS   I suppose so, Mama, but there will always be chickens. You can be sure of that.

EDIE   But suppose someday it happens. Suppose someday there weren't any chickens. Oh, Babs, what could I possibly do? Then the Eggman wouldn't have a job . . . what could I possibly do?

BABS   Now, Mama, that's just egg paranoia. I think you're being very silly. There will always be chickens. Why, there are so many chickens now that we can eat some and let some live in order to supply us with eggs. Chickens are plentiful, Mama. The world will never be without chickens, you can be sure of that.

Crackers enters.

CRACKERS   Afternoon, Ma.

BABS   Hi, honey.

A cloddish mailman wanders onto the trailer lawn, puzzled as to how to deliver his package. He hesitates, then walks to front door and knocks.

Everyone in the trailer jumps up in a panic.

BABS   WHO could that be?!

CRACKERS *(Pulls out his knife)*   I'll be right behind you, Ma. Answer it, it might be nothing.

COTTON *(Peeking out window)*   It's a fucking mailman!

CRACKERS   A mailman? What kind of shit is that? There ain't no address here.

BABS   I'll take care of it. . . . Mother, shut up. Crackers, cover me. Cotton, take that gun. You know how to use it if you have to; right between the eyes.

Cotton takes pistol out of drawer.

Outside of trailer. Mailman begins to knock again when Babs shoves open the front door.

BABS *(Impatiently)*   Yes!?

MAILMAN   Miss Babs Johnson?

BABS   Yes, I'm Babs Johnson.

MAILMAN   Special delivery package, ma'am. Sign here, please.

BABS   What do you mean, special delivery package? There's no address here.

MAILMAN   Says right here—"Babs Johnson, a trailer, Phoenix, Maryland," and you are Babs Johnson, aren't you?

BABS   Of course I'm Babs Johnson! I just told you that! But there is no address here. This is not on any road, route, or street and I don't want people on my property. So don't ever bring mail here again! DO YOU UNDERSTAND?! *(Grabs him by shirt collar)* And the next package you bring me is getting shoved right up your little ass! Can you understand that? *(Shoves him away)* Now, you have exactly fifteen seconds to get off my property, motherfucker, before I break your goddamn neck. *(Mailman starts running)* ONE, ONE THOUSAND! TWO, ONE THOUSAND! THREE, ONE THOUSAND! RUN, YOU BASTARD, RUN.

Interior of trailer. Babs enters carrying package. Cotton and Crackers huddle around her excitedly.

COTTON   Good work, Babs, he ran just like a jackrabbit.

CRACKERS   That was a postman, Ma, I'm sure of that. At least it wasn't no porker. I thought for sure it was the cops.

BABS *(Furious)*   Who could have sent me this package? Who would dare?! *(She begins to open it)* The return address is "The Filthiest People Alive." Who would dare use that title?

COTTON   It's wrapped all fancy, it's just a birthday present, Babs.

BABS   It's no birthday present, Cotton. I smell deep dark trouble.

She opens the package and recoils in horror; inside is a human turd.

BABS OH MY GOD ALMIGHTY, SOMEONE HAS SENT ME A BOWEL MOVEMENT!

COTTON *(Holding her nose)* Oh, Babs!

CRACKERS A turd, Mama, a turd!

COTTON Who could have sent this?

EDIE AHHHH. A turd! Oh, Babs, a turd!

BABS *(In a rage)* This is a direct attack on my Divinity! A direct attack on the peace and harmony of our last few weeks here! An outrageous attempt to humiliate and disgrace my private life! Someone will pay for this; someone will pay with their life for this grossly offensive act!

CRACKERS Mama, nobody sends you a turd and expects to live, NOBODY!

COTTON Look, here's a card.

BABS Read it, Cotton.

COTTON It's a birthday card, a fucking birthday card.

BABS What does it say?!

COTTON Oh, God, Babs. *(She holds it up)* "Happy Birthday, Fatso."

BABS Aaaaaahhhh!

COTTON "You are no longer the filthiest person alive, we are," and it's signed "The Filthiest People Alive."

BABS   Just as I thought, a deliberate attempt to seize my title!

EDIE   The Eggman didn't do it, Babs, I *know* he didn't do it.

BABS   *(Exasperated)* Oh, I don't think he did either, Mother. Just shut up and let me think.

COTTON   That Cookie was asking questions, Crackers, I heard her.

CRACKERS   She's right, Mama. But why would she send us a turd?

BABS   Who knows? These are obviously jealous people; jealous of our careers, of our press. Why else would they sign it "The Filthiest People Alive"? Everyone knows that title has become my trademark. Why, to use it in this way is only to insinuate that they are filthier than I. How could anyone seriously believe that? How could anyone be filthier than Divine? I'm afraid our little vacation must come to an end. This must be nipped in the bud, it's already out of hand. We must outfilth the asshole or assholes who sent this and then THEY MUST DIE!

As we again hear the Narrator's voice, a quick shot of the Marbles' house flashes on screen.

NARRATOR   Connie and Raymond Marble, while you are away, the servants will play!

Shot of Channing sitting at Connie Marble's desk, talking to his reflection in a mirror. He has made himself up in a grotesque parody of Connie, wearing her blue suit and similar makeup, with red poster paint sloppily applied to his hair. He seems to be in a trance and talks with a ridiculous feminine voice.

CHANNING *(Mimicking Connie's earlier scene)* Well, Miss Sandstone, after looking over your qualifications, we've decided you're not exactly what we had in mind. . . .

Raymond and Connie enter downstairs.

CONNIE Where's Channing to help me take off my coat?

RAYMOND You must remember that Channing is not as intelligent as you or I. *(He hears Channing upstairs talking to himself)* Who on earth is that?

CONNIE *(Listening)* It sounds like Channing!

They sneak upstairs and hide outside Connie's office, listening to Channing impersonate them. They become more and more enraged as his words are heard.

CHANNING *(With exaggerated seriousness)* I love you, Raymond. I love you more than anything in this world. I love you more than my own hair color, more than the sound of bones breaking, more than the sound of the death rattle. . . . *(He suddenly changes his voice to a masculine tone and puts a blue mop on his head in obvious imitation of Raymond Marble)* And I too love you, Connie, more than anything I could ever imagine, more than my hair color, or babies screaming or dogs dying. . . .

Connie and Raymond rush into office. Channing cringes in fear.

CONNIE WHAT DO YOU THINK YOU'RE DOING!?

RAYMOND   What is the meaning of this outrage?

CONNIE   Let me at him! I've been waiting to do this for a lifetime! *(She slaps him across the face)*

CHANNING   No, Connie, no!

RAYMOND   How do you dare to be dressed as you are? How do you dare say the things we heard you say?

CHANNING   No, please, listen! I didn't mean any harm.

CONNIE *(Twisting his ear)*   You little asshole, you better start explaining! How dare you go into my personal clothes closet and get my suit? And that's my makeup you have on, isn't it? You sneaky little drag queen! You've been spying on us, haven't you? Huh? Haven't you, aerial ears!?

RAYMOND   Mimicking my wife's hard work and her beautiful appearance! And having the gall to repeat words that Connie and I spoke confidentially. Words that are guarded by the holy seal of matrimony!

CHANNING   I can't help it. I was just playing!

CONNIE   PLAYING? Is that what you'd call it, Channing? Or should I start calling you Connie now? Is that what you'd like?! *(She slaps him again)*

CHANNING *(Crying)*   Stop hitting me. I didn't do anything to you. I was just here by myself and I start feeling funny when I'm alone. Those girls are down there, don't forget. I can't stand being in the same house with them. I can hear them screaming and crying, and then I get all nervous— then I get these spells. I don't plan it, it just happens, and then, well, I think about my position, my social standing, just like you two do, and I just play. I make believe that I *am* you. I know it isn't reality, I know I'm really me. Haven't I been a faithful servant for two years now? Haven't I given you my all in this job?

CONNIE   Oh, you've been faithful all right! Faithful in your stupidity, faithful in your laziness, faithful in your incompetent lame-brain attitude. And now this shockingly flagrant breach of contract! We can no longer employ you here at 3900, Channing, that is obvious. There will be a complete inspection of all your bags, so do not attempt to take anything with you. I will also take a complete inventory of all my belongings from makeup . . . *(Pulls up his skirt)* . . . OH GOD, right on down to panties! And of course have everything sent to the cleaners immediately; God knows what you could have gotten on my clothes. Now, go to your room and STAY THERE until we summon you.

CHANNING   Oh please change your minds. I was only playing . . . I won't . . .

RAYMOND   Stop that yammering and move! And don't try anything funny or you'll be right down there with Suzie and Linda. How would you like that? Had we known, we would have given you a maid's uniform instead of a butler's!

As Channing awkwardly flees the room in Connie's ill-fitting heels, the Marbles break into a shrill, mocking laughter.

Channing clomps down the steps, through the living room and dining room to the closet that he calls his "room." He cries the whole way.

CHANNING *(Mumbling to himself)* Just playing . . . just playing . . . I know I'm not you, Connie . . . it was just playing. *(He takes off Connie's suit and stands in bra and panties)* I wasn't really spying . . . it was just playing . . . oh, what will they do to me? Oh, please let them make me stay. Oh, God have mercy on me.

RAYMOND *(Jumping from behind door to scare him)* NOW WHAT ARE YOU SAYING?

CHANNING Nothing, Raymond, oh God, nothing! I wasn't saying anything.

RAYMOND Connie and I have to go out for a while and we want to make sure that you stay in your room so we're going to lock you in.

CHANNING Lock me in? I won't go anywhere, please!

RAYMOND *(Shuts door and begins locking it)* You shouldn't mind staying in here, Channing. It's rather obvious that you are, to use vulgar slang, a closet queen.

CHANNING *(Muffled)* Please! Don't lock me in! I'll just stay here and be me while you're gone; I won't even think about being you.

≋≋≋

Long shot of the trailer. The Narrator's nagging voice is heard again.

NARRATOR With the shock of the obscene parcel still fresh in their minds, the trailer residents bravely go ahead with their birthday celebration and the Eggman lets his true feel-

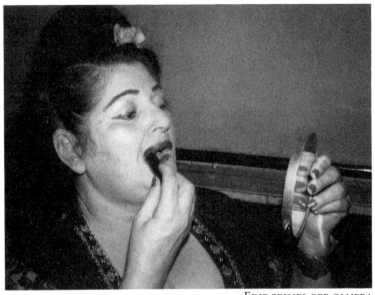

EDIE PRIMPS OFF-CAMERA

ings be known to Edie. Oh happy day! Edie has accepted the Eggman's offer of marriage.

Close-up of Edie and the Eggman kissing. They gaze into each other's eyes like lovebirds.

EDIE   You mean you'll bring me fifty eggs a day? And I can come and visit Babs, and Cotton, and Crackers? And you'll buy me a new girdle and bra and pretty underthings?

EGGMAN   Yes, Edie. Yes, yes, yes. I'll make you the happiest egg lady ever. Don't you worry. I love you. I love you more than anything in this whole world and right after the party you and I are gonna take our first little trip together. I'm going to take you to the largest poultry factory on the East Coast and then you can eat and eat and eat all the eggs you'd ever want.

EDIE   A hundred eggs a day? You mean I could eat a hundred?

EGGMAN   A thousand if you want 'em!

EDIE   I do love you, Mr. Eggman. Even though I do love my little eggies just a little bit better, I do love you more than any MAN I have ever known.

EGGMAN   And I, Edie, love you more than any woman I ever laid eyes on and if you love me just half as much as you love them eggs, then our marriage is just as good as sealed in heaven. *(They kiss again)*

Cut to close-up of birthday cake. "Happy Birthday Babs —The Filthiest Person Alive" is spelled out in icing.

Babs, Crackers, and Cotton stand in receiving line as the guests arrive. Babs wears a white fishtailed evening gown, Cotton wears a white velvet coat, and Crackers has donned a rumpled tie and coat. The guests are a motley collection of hippies, hillbillies, and assorted lunatics.

The guests are seen stuffing their mouths with refreshments, guzzling liquor, and smoking grass.

Connie and Raymond's limousine approaches the trailer.

They get out of car looking very grim and sneak up into the woods to spy on the party.

Babs is seen opening her birthday gifts. She happily unwraps a box of "A-200" crab lice medicine. Cotton gives her a pig's head, Crackers gives her a huge meat cleaver, and one of the guests gives her a box of amyl nitrate. She

PINK FLAMINGOS AND OTHER FILTH

DIVINE AND COTTON AT THE BIRTHDAY PARTY

DIVINE OPENS A PRACTICAL GIFT

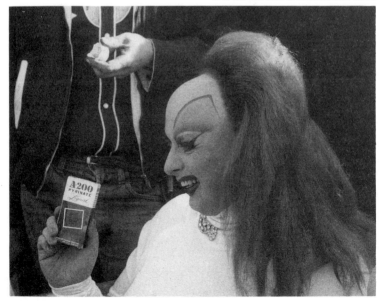

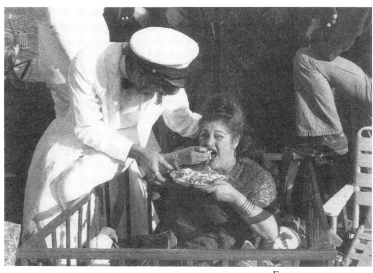

EDIE CHOWS DOWN

RAYMOND AND CONNIE MARBLE (DAVID LOCHARY
AND MINK STOLE) WATCH IN DISGUST

cracks one open, puts it to her nose, and breaks into a drug-induced fit of laughter.

Edie is seen in her party dress still sitting in the playpen. She gorges herself on hard-boiled eggs while babbling to the guests.

A jug band is playing while a snake charmer dances with a boa constrictor.

The guests applaud the entertainment.

A young man walks onto the entertainer's platform nude except for a posing strap. He contorts his body to the enthusiastic cheering of the guests.

He takes off his scanty costume, lies on his back, and throws his legs over his head.

Close-up of his asshole opening and closing in such a way it appears to be singing.

Connie and Raymond look appalled as they continue spying from a nearby clump of bushes.

The guests go wild over the boy with the singing sphincter muscle.

Connie and Raymond can stand no more. They run back to their car and drive away.

A phone booth alongside a country road. Connie and Raymond are both in the booth.

RAYMOND   Hello? . . . Operator, give me the police depart-
ment, please . . . county headquarters.

CONNIE   Phase three, Raymond. Phase three!

RAYMOND   Hello? . . . I'd like to report a lewd and disor-
derly party. . . . No, I'm a neighbor and it's making me
sick. The sight of such perverts guzzling wine and taking
dope right out in the open . . .

CONNIE   Tell them where it is.

RAYMOND   It's on Philpot Road . . . first driveway on the
left . . . walk up into the woods and it's taking place in a
trailer . . . yes, I believe a woman does live there . . . if you
could call her a woman; she is a whore, officer. . . . Yes,
well, when I see these things I feel it's my duty to report
them. . . .

*Two uniformed policemen and two plainclothesmen ap-
proach the trailer. They communicate with walkie-talkies.
The party is still going strong.*

*Crackers spots one of the cops and runs to the party to
alert the drunken guests.*

*The guests rush to hide. Some enter the trailer; some hide
behind it and some on top of it.*

*The cops stand on front lawn, stupidly gawking at what
appears to be an abandoned trailer.*

*All at once the guests charge and attack the startled police-
men with clubs, knives, and guns.*

A young red-haired woman in Nazi outfit shoots one of the cops.

A free-for-all follows. The cops are clubbed unconscious.

The party guests begin to hack and rip apart the policemen's bodies.

Babs rips off the cop's arm and begins eating it. The guests follow her example and soon all the guests are cannibalizing the cops. Blood and guts spill out to the delight of the crazed partygoers.

Quick shots of guests stuffing entrails, livers, etc., into their mouths.

The guests begin to leave, thanking Babs, Crackers, and Cotton for the good time.

We see Edie being lifted into a wheelbarrow. Tin cans and a "Just Engaged" sign decorate the wheelbarrow. The Eggman struggles to lift it and eventually pushes her away. Edie waves good-bye to Babs, Crackers, and Cotton, who seem to be quite moved at seeing Mama Edie leaving them for her honeymoon.

Long shot of a beautiful park. The Marbles' limousine slowly cruises by as we hear the Narrator.

NARRATOR   Even with the hectic events of the day, Raymond Marble still finds time to satisfy his perverted urges. Watch, as he not only commits another act of indecent exposure, but adds to this social horror by making his wife wait in the car! Is there no shame?!

PINK FLAMINGOS

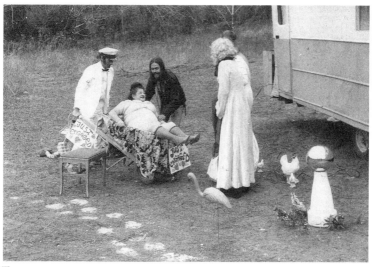

THE HONEYMOON BEGINS . . .

. . . ON A CHILLY WINTER DAY

Shot of beautiful young woman sitting in park applying makeup.

Raymond Marble sneaks up and flashes his penis at her. A turkey neck is tied to the end of it.

The young woman laughs, opens the top of her dress, and fondles her large breasts at him.

Shocked, Raymond shakes his penis and turkey neck at her more violently.

Still undaunted, the young woman pulls up her dress to reveal "her" penis and begins shaking it back at Raymond.

The sight of the woman with beautiful breasts and a penis is too much for Raymond. He looks completely horrified and runs back to his car as the young woman laughs at him.

Interior of Marbles' living room.

NARRATOR   This is not the only shock you have before you, Raymond Marble, because at this exact moment Divine has learned of your jealous scheme from the local town gossip. She also has your address, ASSHOLE!

Babs and Crackers break in the front door. Babs is carrying a gun and looks eager to use it. She wears a skintight royal blue jumpsuit and spike heels.

BABS   Connie! Raymond!

CRACKERS   They're probably hiding their asses.

BABS   It would be a prudent move on their part if they were, but I could smell 'em if they were here. Come on, let's go upstairs. *(They creep up steps)* CONNIE, YOU HAVE COMPANY!

CRACKERS   We got something here for you.

They enter bedroom and sit on the bed.

CRACKERS   Echhh! Their bedroom! Their fuck chamber itself!

BABS   This is where they mate, Crackers. Right here on this very bed! This is why they touch their uninspired little organs together, vainly trying to recharge their worn-out battery of filthiness, thrashing and moaning in the still of the night. *(She begins licking everything in the room)*

CRACKERS   *(Also beginning to lick objects)*   What kind of shit turns them on, Mama? What do they do in here?

BABS   Oh, all sorts of disgusting positions I would imagine, Crackers. Connie probably takes Raymond's little peanut of a cock between her brittle chapped lips and then scrapes her ugly decayed teeth up and down on it while asshole Raymond thinks he's getting the best head on the East Coast. Then they probably sit here and stare at each other's blue and red hair while they goose each other and say dirty words. *(She continues to lick the furniture)* Get everything real good, honey!

Babs and Crackers descend the steps to living room, licking and sucking the banister the whole way.

They enter living room, moaning with passion and continuing their plan to suck the whole house.

BABS   Oh, Crackers, get this couch real good! *(They both sit on couch and lick it)* They probably sit here and say all sorts of banal things to each other. Why, they may have even decided to send us that turd on this very sofa.

CRACKERS *(Licking and drooling)*   I'm getting it all, Mama, don't you worry! They think they're filthier. We'll just see what the furniture thinks, right, Ma? Am I right?

BABS   Yes, Crackers! Don't miss anything!

CRACKERS   Should I shit on the floor, Mama? Right here in the living room?

BABS   No, not yet. Just get your saliva glands going. *(Spittle pours out of Babs' mouth)* JUICY!

CRACKERS   Is it enough? Shouldn't we do something a little filthier, a little heavier?

BABS *(Jumping up)*   We still have other rooms to go! THE DINING ROOM!

They rush into dining room and frantically begin to lick the table, plates, and silverware.

BABS   This is where they eat, Crackers. This is where they shove dirty little pieces of bacteria down their weaselly little throats. This is where they spread germs, disease, and infection—gobbling obscene fruits and vegetables all in the name of health. How disgusting! Get this table soaking wet!

CRACKERS   Oh, Mama, Mama, this is going to work. Our Divinity will show through all the bullshit crammed into this little dwelling. The house WILL react, Mama.

BABS   Oh, Crackers, my little baby, Crackers. No house could stand the two of our venoms, our saliva. It will work! Oh, my only son, Crackers!

They move to couch in dining room.

CRACKERS   Mama! Mama! I just thank God above I was lucky enough to be the soul that was placed in my body; the body of Divine's son! The body and blood of another generation of Divinity. *(He starts rubbing his crotch)*

BABS   My only baby, Crackers! My own flesh and blood, my own heritage, my own genes. Let Mama receive you like Communion. Let Mama make a gift to you, a gift so special it will curse this house years after we're gone. Oh, Crackers, a gift of supreme mothergood, a gift of DIVIN-ITY! *(She falls to the floor)*

CRACKERS   *(Rubbing his crotch and moaning)*   I want to accept your gift, accept it as a loving son should—a son that would kill for you, steal for you, even die for you, Mama. Oh yes, I accept your gift *(Unzips his pants)*, accept it as a loving son should. I'm yours, completely yours!

BABS   Crackers, prepare to receive the most divine gift a mother can give. *(She begins to blow him)*

CRACKERS   Oh MAMA! This will clinch it! This will ruin this house forever! That's it, that's it! Do my balls, Mama! That's it! Ahhhhh! Further down! Oh, Mama, you're the best, the best ever. I should have known you'd be better than anyone!

Offscreen we hear the muffled cries of Channing.

Babs jumps up in a panic, leaving Crackers on the couch still sexually aroused.

BABS   Crackers, somebody else is in here!

CRACKERS   But, Mama, Mama. God damn it!

BABS   Get your gun!

CRACKERS *(Struggling with his pants)*   God damn it!

Interior of trailer. Connie and Raymond are carrying a red gas can and begin pouring the gas over the furniture.

RAYMOND   This place ought to go up like a tinderbox. Spread it everywhere.

RAYMOND TORCHES THE TRAILER

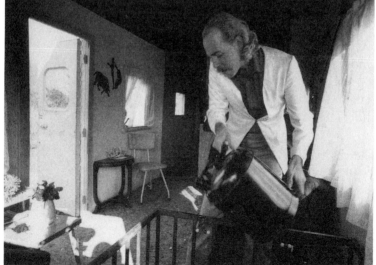

CONNIE   God, I love the smell of gasoline, Raymond. We ARE the filthiest people alive!

RAYMOND   As we always have been, Connie. Revenge, oh sweet revenge. Wonder how that fat cow likes prison?

CONNIE   Probably couldn't fit the son in a cell with anyone else. I wonder how her party guests like her now. I wonder if she had a happy birthday.

RAYMOND   Let's hurry and get out of here. You know how fire makes me nervous.

CONNIE   Nonsense, Raymond. Fire is beautiful; licking and scorching everything it touches. *(Pointing to kitchen counter)* Get some more on here. Get their bedrooms!

Babs and Crackers stand outside Channing's closet after discovering him.

CRACKERS   Who else is in this house? Where's everyone else hiding?

CHANNING *(Shaking with fear)*   Just the girls. Please don't hurt me, I won't call the police.

BABS   You're goddamn right you won't! Now, where are Connie and Raymond Marble?

CHANNING   They went out, I swear. Just the girls are here— the girls in the cellar.

CRACKERS   What girls?!

CHANNING The girls they keep locked up. Please let me go. You can do anything you like but please just let me out of this house.

BABS When will the Marbles be back? TELL US! *(Slaps Channing)*

CHANNING *(Crying)* I don't know. They locked me in here this morning after they fired me. Just let me out of this house.

BABS *(Grabbing Channing by the arm)* Come on, we'll go see about these girls you keep talking about.

Channing, Crackers, and Babs enter the Marbles' torture pit. Suzie and Linda jump up in confusion.

SUZIE *(Startled)* Oh, please help us! What is this? Please . . . please . . .

LINDA Call the police! Contact my parents! Please . . . take them this note, the address is on the back.

BABS Where are Connie and Raymond Marble?

CRACKERS What is this shit?

LINDA How would I know? I've been locked up here. I never saw them except for the day they kidnapped me. We never see them—only Channing.

SUZIE Please help us to escape. *(To Babs, falling to her knees)* Oh, Miss Lady or whoever you are, I beg of you to free Linda and I from here. Please! So I can have an abortion before it's too late. . . .

LINDA   If you free us, we will do anything.

BABS   The Marbles locked you down here?

SUZIE   Yes, I've been here for months. Endless horror-filled months in this damp pit, chained like a starving animal, only hoping that I would be killed rather than continue living like this.

CRACKERS   You never see the Marbles? Never?

LINDA   No! Only Channing, this repulsive pervert you have tied up. Please, he raped us both so we would become pregnant.

SUZIE   The Marbles just sit up there waiting for us to die in childbirth. Then they sell the poor babies; it's been a night-

THE PIT

mare! If you don't free us, we will die and rot in this pit. They have no mercy.

BABS   Free them, Crackers.

LINDA   Channing's got the key in his pocket!

CHANNING   Let me go! I didn't do anything!

BABS   Shut up, filthy bastard.

SUZIE   Don't let him go, Miss Lady. He has beaten me many times and caused me untold misery.

LINDA   He's one of them. He works for the Marbles.

CHANNING   I was only doing my job. I have no malice towards either of you.

CRACKERS *(Unchaining Linda)*   There you go, honey.

LINDA   Thank you. Oh, God, I can go home again.

CRACKERS *(Freeing Suzie)*   There you go, missy, free as a bird.

SUZIE   Oh, thank you, so very much. Could we chain him? *(Looks over at Channing)*

BABS   Do whatever you like. You can even kill him if you want. Either you do it or we will.

LINDA & SUZIE   Let us! Let us!

SUZIE *(Picks up knife and approaches Channing)*   Well, Channing, the tables turn, don't they?

CHANNING   Please, Suzie! I couldn't free you. Have mercy on me!

SUZIE   You kept us locked up like slaves, bastard, and you're going to pay for it. I'm gonna cut that big fat worm right off you.

CHANNING   No! Oh God, NO! NOT THAT!

Tight close-up of Babs and Crackers climbing up ladder out of pit. They have a twisted smile on their faces as we hear offscreen Linda and Suzie's revenge.

SUZIE   Want to jerk off one more time, stud?

LINDA   HOLD HIM!

CHANNING   NO!

REVENGE IS SWEET

LINDA THERE, I'VE GOT IT! CUT IT!

CHANNING AHHHHHH . . .

A look of contentment and joy comes over Babs' and Crackers' faces as they exit the pit.

Raymond and Connie stand outside the trailer. Connie holds a gasoline-soaked torch.

RAYMOND Light it, my darling.

CONNIE We ARE the filthiest people alive! *(She lights the torch)* Fire, fire, burn it down, fire, fire, to the ground! *(She turns the torch into living room of trailer and the fire quickly spreads)* Burn, you fucker! Burn!

RAYMOND Someone will see the smoke. Hurry! It's done! The Battle of Filth has been won!

CONNIE *(Laughing insanely as they run away)* WE ARE THE FILTHIEST PEOPLE ALIVE!

Fire quickly spreads throughout the trailer. Smoke pours from the windows.

Rear view of the trailer. Blazing furniture is seen as the back porch crumbles in flames.

Close-up of melted plastic pink flamingos on front lawn.

Long shot of the entire trailer burning out of control.

Babs, Crackers, and Cotton stroll up the path through the woods to the trailer.

BABS Goddamn Marbles!

CRACKERS We'll take care of them.

COTTON We'll get those assholes later.

CRACKERS *(Suddenly)* Mama! Look, there's smoke! *(They all begin to run)*

BABS Oh, my God!

COTTON The trailer!

They rush to rear of burning trailer but the heat keeps them from approaching too closely. They fall to the ground sobbing.

BABS My gorgeous hideaway! Oh NO, NO, NO!

COTTON All our gorgeous antiques! Our priceless theatrical wardrobe!

CRACKERS THEY did it, them fucking Marbles did it!

BABS *(Dragging Cotton and Crackers away)* BACK! BACK! THE MARBLES! BACK TO THE MARBLES AND SEIZE THOSE FUCKERS! I'LL KILL 'EM!!!

The flames begin to die down and nothing is left but a shell of their home.

A gust of wind hits what is left of the trailer and it collapses in a pile of burning rubble.

Connie and Raymond, out of breath, excited, enter their living room.

CONNIE   At last it is over, Raymond. The Battle of Filth has been won. This calls for a celebration.

RAYMOND   A victory celebration.

CONNIE   Oh, Jesus God, I love you, Raymond. Are you happy with our filthiness, my darling? Are you glad your wife is here beside you sharing with you this bond of filth?

RAYMOND   This has been the most important day of my life. Filthiness is a reality. After all these years of nagging uncertainty, I know that we are indeed the filthiest couple alive. *(They kiss passionately)*

CONNIE   *(Crossing room to lie on couch with outstretched arms)*   Come to me, my darling. Come receive what was promised you in the holy vows of matrimony. I am yours, Raymond, all yours, my beautiful darling.

The three cushions of the couch fly up like a jack-in-the-box, throwing Connie to the floor.

CONNIE   Ahhhhh!

RAYMOND   *(Rushing to help her)*   Connie, are you all right?

CONNIE   *(Terrified)*   What happened, Raymond?

RAYMOND   The couch . . . it . . . it rejected you.

CONNIE   Something's wrong, Raymond. Something's terribly wrong.

RAYMOND   It's just out of order, you're all right—get up.

CONNIE   I'm afraid to, honey. How can a couch be out of order?

RAYMOND   Something just went wrong. *(He sits in chair)* See, this chair is okay.

CONNIE   But that couch *threw* me! Nothing can be wrong with that couch, we just got it!

RAYMOND   It's okay. . . . *(Suddenly the seat of his chair flings him out of it and onto the floor)* Ahhhh!

CONNIE   Raymond!

RAYMOND   I'm all right, I'm not hurt.

CONNIE   Something is the matter with this house! Channing must have done something.

RAYMOND   We'll beat it out of him!

They get up and run through dining room as the dining room table flips itself over with a horrible crash.

The Marbles scream and run in horror.

They run into kitchen and discover Channing's open closet door.

RAYMOND   He's gone! Channing has escaped.

CONNIE   Raymond, check the pit! He may have let the girls go!

They run down steps to the torture pit.

CONNIE   Oh, my God, the police!

Quick shot of Channing's body. He is dead and has been castrated. His crotch is covered in blood.

Connie and Raymond rush to pit and recoil in shock at the sight.

CONNIE   He's been castrated! HIS PENIS IS GONE!

RAYMOND   The girls have escaped. They'll call the police! *(They run back up steps)*

CHANNING'S (CHANNING WILROY) JUST DESERTS

CONNIE   Raymond, I'm afraid.

Quick shot of the living room furniture with its cushions flipping up and down, ridiculously defying its owners to sit on them.

The living room. Babs, Crackers, and Cotton wait by the door in ambush. They are holding guns, knives, and rope.

Connie and Raymond rush in, trying to escape their cursed house, and are seized by Babs and her companions.

BABS   CONNIE AND RAYMOND MARBLE!

CRACKERS *(To Connie)*   You're gonna get it good, bitch.

Crackers holds Connie at knife point and Cotton points a gun at Raymond.

BABS   Well, well, well, Connie and Raymond Marble! I've been looking forward to meeting you. It's a real pleasure. You're even bigger assholes than I had imagined. YOU BURNED MY HOUSE DOWN!

CONNIE   No, please, who are you? We don't know you.

BABS *(Smacks her)*   You know who I am, bitch. I'm the filthiest person alive, that's who I am.

RAYMOND   You must be mistaken, our name is Waldo— Harry and Jean Waldo.

BABS *(In a rage)*   SHUT UP! JUST SHUT UP! *(To Crackers and Cotton)* Gag 'em before I kill 'em.

CRACKERS   Wait for the newsmen, Ma.

COTTON *(Gagging Raymond)* That ought to shut him up. Hey, Raymond, you must think we're awful fucking stupid, huh? *(Starts viciously kicking him)* Here's a little something for you!

CONNIE Who are you! You have the wrong people!

BABS Shut up, Connie, SHUT UP! You know who we are. Cut the hogwash, save it for the papers. You're Connie Marble and you're gonna pay for being Connie Marble! *(Tapes her mouth)* And you're gonna pay royally, bitch. Let this be a lesson to you just in case there *is* reincarnation: it's virtually impossible to be filthier than Divine! I didn't get my reputation for nothing, you know. But you found out too late, Connie, yes too late, because you and shithead here ain't gonna be around for tomorrow. 'Cause you're gonna be dead, Connie, YES DEAD!

COTTON *(Tying up Raymond)* That's tight, Crackers. It's so tight it makes their blood hurt.

BABS Just make sure they don't make another sound, because I don't think I'll be able to control myself if they make any more noise! I would just have to kill them right now, I wouldn't be able to wait!

COTTON I know what you mean, Babs! I feel like ripping them apart myself.

BABS *(Dragging the Marbles across the room)* Come on, children. We can't keep the photographers waiting. We're going to give them a story that will knock the news day right off its fucking boring little ass. *(Pushing the Marbles out the front door)* Come on, Connie and Raymond, you have a personal appearance to make.

Babs, Crackers, and Cotton exit Crackers' shed with Connie and Raymond Marble, who are still tied and gagged. The trailer lies in ruin in front of them. Babs wears a bright red fishtail evening gown. A podium has been set up for the following press conference.

Enter Ron Vespo, a reporter. He carries a tape recorder.

RON VESPO *(Talking into microphone)*   Ron Vespo of *Midnite* here, looking for Divine somewhere in Phoenix, Maryland. *(He sees her)* Divine, you're looking fantastic!

BABS   Well, thank you, Mr. Vespo. I'm so glad you could come.

READY FOR THE PRESS IN A GROUP PRODUCTION STILL
(THAT'S ME, SECOND FROM RIGHT)

Enter another reporter, Mat Hinlin.

MAT HINLIN   Mat Hinlin here from *The Tattler*.

BABS   Good afternoon, Mr. Hinlin. Gentlemen, get ready. You are about to witness the trial of these two unfortunates commonly known as Connie and Raymond Marble. Their trial will take place in front of your very eyes and their execution will follow.

MAT HINLIN *(Incredulously)*   We're going to witness an actual murder?

RON VESPO   A live homicide?

BABS   That is right, gentlemen.

A third reporter approaches.

MOREY ROBERTS   Roberts. Morey Roberts. Very tempting. And I have a question for you, Miss . . . Cotton? Is that correct, "Cotton"?

COTTON   Yes, it is.

MOREY ROBERTS   Are you a willing accomplice to these murders that are about to take place?

COTTON   This is not exactly a murder, Mr. Roberts. This is a court, a kangaroo court, as the headlines could scream. Not a mere murder. If we were involved in merely another murder, it could hardly be headlines.

CRACKERS   It's not just the publicity. My mama couldn't go on with her everyday life with this shit going on. She was

COTTON AND CRACKERS: WITNESSES FOR THE PROSECUTION

not the aggressor in this little war we had; it was suicide on their part.

MAT HINLIN   And Cotton . . . I notice a smile on your lips. Does murder make you happy?

COTTON   Murder merely relieves tension, Mr. Hinlin. For murder to bring happiness, one must already be happy and I am—completely at peace with myself, totally happy.

BABS   Give me more questions!

MAT HINLIN   Divine, are you a lesbian?

BABS   Yes. I have done everything.

RON VESPO   Does blood turn you on?

BABS   It does more than turn me on, Mr. Vespo, it makes me come. And more than the sight of it, I love the taste of it, the taste of hot freshly killed blood.

MOREY ROBERTS   Could you give us some of your political beliefs?

BABS   Kill everyone now! Condone first-degree murder! Advocate cannibalism! Eat shit! Filth is my politics, filth is my life! *(Posing wildly)* Take whatever you like! *(She puts hands on crotch and mugs hideously to the cameramen)* How's this for a center spread?

RON VESPO *(Snaps photo)*   Christ almighty. Okay, Divine, where will you go now? I'm sure you're aware that after the execution you will be the subject of an extensive search.

BABS   To another city to set up headquarters once again. Of course I cannot reveal to you the exact location. Patience, Mr. Vespo, patience. Another time, another story. AND NOW FOR THE TRIAL!!

The newsmen sit on the ground and Connie and Raymond are pushed over next to the podium. Babs steps behind the podium to address the press.

COTTON *(To press)*   You sit here. Sit down. No pictures during the trial, please. This is a court of law.

BABS   I call to the stand Miss Cotton. *(Cotton approaches podium)* Do you solemnly swear to tell the truth, the whole truth, and nothing but the truth?

A CENTERFOLD?

PINK FLAMINGOS

COTTON   I do.

BABS   Who burned down our trailer?

COTTON   Connie and Raymond Marble.

BABS   Can you point them out in this court?

COTTON   There they are right there, the ones that are tied up.

Connie and Raymond shake their heads negatively and their muffled cries can be heard through their gags.

BABS   Who sent me a turd in the mail?

COTTON   Connie and Raymond Marble.

BABS   That is all. *(Looking at the Marbles)* Is there any cross-examination? *(The Marbles try to get free of their restraints, moaning and shaking their heads affirmatively)* No cross-examination? Very well. *(To Cotton)* You may step down. I call to the stand Crackers. *(He approaches podium)* Do you solemnly swear to tell the truth, the whole truth, and nothing but the truth?

CRACKERS   Sure, Mama. I wouldn't shit you.

BABS   How did Connie and Raymond find out where w' lived?

CRACKERS   They hired a spy.

BABS   How did this spy get the information?

CRACKERS By nosing around and by fucking me, that's how she got it. That dirty little scag.

BABS Thank you. *(To the Marbles)* Is there any cross-examination? *(Once again they struggle and whimper but are ignored)* No? A very strange defense, I must say. *(To press)* Gentlemen, the verdict is guilty on all ten counts of first-degree stupidity. The penalty phase will now begin. I call Cotton to the stand. *(Cotton returns to the podium)* Your oath still remains. I presume you understand this?

COTTON Naturally.

BABS In your opinion, what should the penalty in this case be?

COTTON Death.

BABS That is all, you may step down. *(She does)* I call Crackers to the stand. *(He enters)* You realize you are still under oath?

CRACKERS Of course.

BABS In your opinion, should these people be allowed to live?

CRACKERS No.

BABS Thank you. *(Crackers steps down)* *(To press)* Gentlemen of the press, the verdict is death. But first, due to the magnitude of these capital crimes, these two people must be humiliated in front of the media. Use these pictures, gentlemen, and use them wisely. We have an example to set. Let the good people of this country know that they cannot fuck with Divine and get away with it. Let them know that we are indeed the filthiest couple alive! *(The press begins raising their hands wildly to question her)* Mr. Vespo?

RON VESPO   Yes, Divine, do you think there are other filthy people in the world? Is it now a cult?

BABS   It is a very minor cult right now but one that is growing and growing. I will be queen one day and my coronation will be celebrated all over the world! Do not forget, I AM DIVINE!

COTTON   What a day for an execution!

CRACKERS   Off the record, Mama, do we shoot 'em or stab 'em?

BABS   Shoot, Crackers, shoot. No mess for *Midnite.*

MAT HINLIN   Don't forget *The Tattler.*

BABS   And *The Tattler,* honey.

MOREY ROBERTS   And *Confidential.*

BABS   How could I ever forget *Confidential?*

Babs leads the way into the woods. Crackers shoves the Marbles along and Cotton carries a bucket of tar. The press eagerly follows, snapping photos.

BABS   Right this way, gentlemen! Come on!

PINK FLAMINGOS

COTTON   Come on, help me with this tar.

CRACKERS   Okay, Miss Cotton.

Connie and Raymond are tied to a tree. Crackers smears tar over them with a brush. Cotton holds a bag of feathers. Babs and the newsmen stand nearby.

CRACKERS *(Slopping tar on Raymond)*   Burn my mama's house down, will you? You goddamn worm, fucking piece of lousy shit!

BABS   And now for the feathers! *(Cotton and Crackers throw feathers on them)* Only we're not going to run you out of town, we're going to kill you! Kill, kill, kill. Shoot, shoot, shoot. *(To press)* Questions and answers!

MAT HINLIN   Do you believe in God?

MOVING IN FOR A TIGHT SHOT

BABS   I am God.

COTTON *(Giggling, pointing to Crackers)*   You are God.

CRACKERS *(Pointing to Cotton)*   You are God.

MOREY ROBERTS   Is there no wrong?

BABS   There is right and there is wrong. *I* have never been wrong, Mr. Roberts.

MAT HINLIN   Do you expect to get new followers from this publicity?

BABS   I certainly hope so. I didn't invite you here to jerk off, you know. Get this all down! Don't miss one single word!

FILMING *PINK FLAMINGOS*

RON VESPO   Suppose we decide not to print this story, what then?

BABS   Ha! *(Pointing to the Marbles)* See them? Does that answer your question? I have your address and I know you have a wife and child, is that correct?

RON VESPO   Yes.

BABS   Well, if nothing is printed, we might be in the mood for a barbecue. Get what I mean? A human barbecue! END OF QUESTION-AND-ANSWER PERIOD! PROCEED WITH THE EXECUTION! *(She aims a pistol)* They are finished and a lovely couple they are, aren't they? Gentlemen of the press, get ready. You are about to witness the biggest news event of the year: live homicide! *(Approaching the Marbles with pistol aimed)* Connie and Raymond Marble, you have breathed your last breath, you have sighed your last sigh. You are no longer alive! *(She*

THE HAPPY FAMILY

shoots Raymond right between his eyes) Connie Marble, you stand convicted of assholism! The proper punishment will now take place. Look pretty for the picture, Connie. That's it! *(She shoots Connie in the forehead) (Close-up of the Marbles, dead, tarred and feathered)* No further questions, no further pictures. *I* have spoken! *(The newsmen begin to leave)*

RON VESPO   Thanks for the scoop, Divine. Next month's sales should be booming.

BABS   Thank you for coming.

MAT HINLIN   *(To the other journalists)*   You can always count on her for a story.

RON VESPO   She always was a news-conscious woman. Only problem is, we've been trying to get *Midnite* into the supermarkets and this is a hot story all right, but it's so squalid.

MAT HINLIN   Yeah, well *The Tattler*'ll be in the supermarkets, you can bet on that.

Babs, Crackers, and Cotton relax under a tree near the execution site.

BABS   The time has come for flight, my children.

CRACKERS   Where to, Mama, where to?

COTTON   Let's move to Boise, I always wanted to go there.

BABS   Boise, Cotton? Why, that might not be a bad idea.

PINK FLAMINGOS AND OTHER FILTH

CRACKERS   Were you ever there, Cotton?

COTTON   Only once. We robbed a transit bus there, remember?

BABS   I remember, the number forty-two.

CRACKERS   Let's sleep in gas-station lavatories this time, Mama. Fuck permanent residences. It'll strengthen our filthiness.

COTTON   Crackers, that's a wonderful idea. What do you say, Babs, let's move to Boise.

BABS   If that's what you want, my children, then that's what you'll get. Boise, Idaho, here we come! I hope Boise's ready for some star residents. Why, I'll have to change my appearance. I think I'll dye my hair another color and start dressing like a dyke.

COTTON   Me, too. I'll get a crew cut.

CRACKERS   Maybe it's about time I started dying my hair too.

BABS   What color do you want, honey? I'm gonna make mine hot pink with a DA and Elvis Presley sideburns.

CRACKERS   Maybe blond, Mama. Do you think I'd look good as a blond? Do you think it would enhance my filthiness?

COTTON   You *should* dye your hair. It would make you look much filthier. Oh, won't it be fun? I'll have a crew cut, you'll have a pink DA, and Crackers will have blond hair, all in Boise, Idaho!

PINK FLAMINGOS

BABS   Then it's settled. Boise, Idaho, get ready! You are about to receive some migrants of a very special nature, a nature that defies description. You are about to receive into your community the filthiest people alive!

Babs, Crackers, and Cotton walking up a city street carrying suitcases. Crackers has a sign saying "Boise."

NARRATOR   The filthiest people alive? Well, you think you know someone filthier? Watch, as Divine proves that not only is she the filthiest person in the world, she is also the filthiest actress in the world! What you are about to see is THE REAL THING!

"BOISE, IDAHO, GET READY!"

PINK FLAMINGOS AND OTHER FILTH

As they continue walking, a boy passes, walking a Hungarian sheepdog.

They break into a broad grin and Babs rubs her stomach.

The final take is one medium shot without cuts. Babs rushes over to the dog as it takes a shit. She scoops up the shit and puts it in her mouth. She rolls it around on her tongue and gags and winks at the camera. Zoom in on Babs giving a shit-eating grin to the camera and the audience.

T H E   E N D

DIVINE AND MINK, OFF-CAMERA

OPENING NIGHT AT THE ELGIN IN NEW YORK;
INCORRECT TITLE ON MARQUEE

Desperate
ᐳLivingᐸ

MOLE AND MUFFY (SUSAN LOWE AND LIZ RENAY)

DESPERATE LIVING
WRITTEN, DIRECTED, AND FILMED BY JOHN WATERS

Cast

Muffy St. Jacques	LIZ RENAY
Peggy Gravel	MINK STOLE
Mole McHenry	SUSAN LOWE
Queen Carlotta	EDITH MASSEY
Princess Coo-Coo	MARY VIVIAN PEARCE
Grizelda Brown	JEAN HILL
Flipper	COOKIE MUELLER
Shina	MARINA MELIN
Shotsie	SHARON NIESP
Lt. Wilson	ED PERANIO
Lt. Grogan	STEVE BUTOW
Lt. Williams	CHANNING WILROY
Bosley Gravel	GEORGE STOVER
Motorcycle Cop	TURKEY JOE
Muffy's Husband	ROLAND HERTZ
Baby-sitter	PIRIE WOODS
Big Jimmy Dong	H. C. KLIEMISCH
Herbert	GEORGE FIGGS
Pervert	PAT MORAN
Nurse	DELORES DELUXE
Goons	PETER KOPER, STEVE PARKER, CHUCK YEATON, PETE DENZER, RALPH CROCKER, DAVID KLEIN

Art Director   VINCENT PERANIO
Costumes and Makeup   VAN SMITH
Director of Photography   THOMAS LOIZEAUX
Sound   ROBERT MAIER
Editor   CHARLES ROGGERO
Music   COMPOSED AND ARRANGED BY
CHRIS LOBINGIER AND ALLEN YARUS

Opening credits are superimposed over elegant dinner table. A pair of black hands sets the table and pours some wine. Another course is served—this time a boiled rat heavily garnished. A pair of white hands with knife and fork enters the frame, cuts rat, and spears hunks of rat meat. Finally, the fork is set down and a rat bone is placed on center of plate.

Dissolve to shot of upper-class home. Shot of Grizelda, 350-pound maid, vacuuming. Children are playing ball. Bosley Gravel, thirty-five, cloddish, and preppy, is seen talking to distinguished psychiatrist.

DOCTOR   You must realize, Bosley, your wife is one of the most neurotic women I've ever examined. I still think a few more months in the sanitarium would be helpful. It may be too early to trust her in her natural environment.

BOSLEY   Oh, Doc, be optimistic! Peggy's breakdown is part of the past now. I don't want her in another mental hospital, I want her home with me and the kids. Dr. Evans, the road to mental health is just around the corner.

Shot of kids still playing baseball.

One hits a ball through window.

Interior Peggy Gravel's bedroom. She is polishing her nails and always seems on the verge of a fit. She wears a leg brace. As ball crashes through her window, she lets out a shriek.

PEGGY   I knew they'd try it. Trying to kill me in my own home! *(Staggering toward window)* It's like WAR! Don't tell me I don't know what Vietnam is like! *(Opening window and yelling)* BRATS! BRATS! BRATS!

Shot of stunned kids looking up.

BOSLEY JR.   Oh, Mom!

KID   I'm sorry, Mrs. Gravel, I'll pay for the window out of my allowance.

PEGGY GRAVEL (MINK STOLE)

PEGGY   How about my life? Do you get enough allowance to pay for that?! I know you were trying to kill me! What's the matter with the courts!? Do they allow this lawlessness and malicious destruction of property to run rampant?! I hate the Supreme Court! *(She smashes vase) (She leans back out window)* Go home to your mother! Doesn't she ever watch you?! Tell her this isn't some Communist day-care center! Tell your mother I hate her! Tell your mother I hate YOU!

Phone rings.

PEGGY *(Continuing)*   Hello . . . *(Furious)* WHAT NUMBER ARE YOU CALLING!? . . . YOU'VE DIALED THE WRONG NUMBER!! . . . SORRY!?? WHAT GOOD IS THAT!? HOW CAN YOU EVER REPAY THE THIRTY SECONDS YOU'VE STOLEN FROM MY LIFE!? I HATE YOU, YOUR HUSBAND, YOUR CHILDREN, AND YOUR RELATIVES!

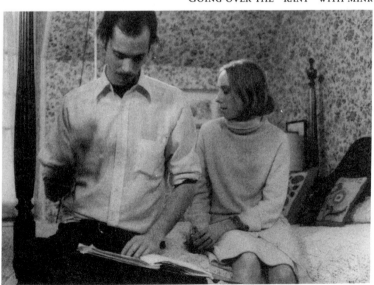

GOING OVER THE "RANT" WITH MINK

She slams down phone and exits.

She limps down the steps.

PEGGY *(Sobbing)* God . . . God . . . God . . . What did I do to deserve this!?

Grizelda, the 350-pound maid, rushes out.

GRIZELDA Miss Gravel, what's the matter? You having another fit?

PEGGY Can't my husband keep an eye on the children? Can't that lazy moron do one thing!?

GRIZELDA The kids are just outside, they're okay. Let me get you some of your fit medicine.

PEGGY *(Crying uncontrollably)* Grizelda, my life is in danger. *(Hugging her)* Please don't let anyone hurt me. *(Sobbing)*

GRIZELDA There. There. You gotta keep calm, woman. You're imagining things.

PEGGY That's what you think! One of the neighborhood children just tried to murder me. I was sitting in my bedroom applying nail polish and he fired a rifle at me!

GRIZELDA Oh, Miss Gravel!

PEGGY It's true! I must get the children before they're kidnapped! *(She rushes out)*

GRIZELDA *(Shaking her head)* Good God almighty.

PEGGY *(Walking to attic) (Frantically)* Beth!? . . . Bosley Jr.?!!

Shot of kids in attic. They are nude, innocently playing doctor. Bosley Jr. examines Beth with a toy stethoscope.

BOSLEY JR.   Breathe hard. *(She does)* Do it again.

BETH *(Giggles as she breathes)*   Let me do it to you.

Peggy enters and goes berserk when she sees them.

PEGGY   SODOMITES! *(She rushes to them)* CAUGHT RIGHT IN A SEX ORGY! FILTHY! DIRTY! FILTHY!

BOSLEY JR. *(Crying)*   We're only playing.

PEGGY *(Slapping them)*   Is that what you learned in private school!!?

BETH   Don't, Mother, we're only playing!

PEGGY *(Hysterically to herself)*   NUDE! NUDE! NUDE! *(Suddenly seriously)* You could be pregnant, Beth! *(To Bosley Jr.)* And YOU. . . . I never thought you'd rape your own sister! *(Suddenly wildly, to no one in particular)* OH GOD, THE CHILDREN ARE HAVING SEX!!

Shot of Bosley, in living room, reading the Wall Street Journal. *He hears Peggy shrieking in background and gets up to go check it out.*

Bosley enters kitchen. Grizelda is drinking liquor out of a fifth.

BOSLEY   Where's Peg— *(Sees Grizelda)* *(Sarcastically)* THIRSTY, GRIZELDA??

Grizelda puts down bottle, wipes her mouth, and ignores him.

GRIZELDA *(Doing chores suddenly)*   You better see about your wife, she's having one of her mental fits.

BOSLEY   I thought you had been stealing my liquor!

GRIZELDA   Ain't nobody stealing nothing from you, Mr. Gravel.

BOSLEY   We'll see about that! *(He goes over to liquor cabinet and pulls out a fifth)* You didn't know I marked these, did you? Here. Look here. See this pencil line? That was marked just yesterday. You've had quite a few *cocktails*, haven't you? *(Grizelda picks up her purse)* What else have you pilfered, Grizelda? I think I'll have a look in that purse.

GRIZELDA   You ain't lookin' in my purse.

BOSLEY   Why not? Got something to hide?

GRIZELDA   Don't you know men aren't supposed to look in a lady's handbag?

BOSLEY   *Lady?!* YOU'RE FIRED, GRIZELDA! No wonder you people are always in the unemployment line. NOW, GIVE ME THAT BAG!

GRIZELDA *(Struggling)*   I don't want no white man lookin' at my Tampax!

BOSLEY *(Grabbing her bag and going through it)* I wouldn't worry about your Tampax if I were you! . . . WELL, look at this! . . . My savings account book . . . WITH withdrawal slips . . . my lottery tickets . . . and two rolls of toilet paper! *(Grabbing her arm)* I'm now placing you under citizen's arrest. I'm going to call the police and report you!

GRIZELDA Get off me, milk head.

Peggy comes running in hysterically.

PEGGY *(Seeing Bosley)* I see you're finally here! It's a little late, isn't it? The children are having sex. Beth is pregnant. I narrowly escaped assassination a few moments ago. Will you please do something!

BOSLEY *(Trying to hug her)* Ah, honey. It's just your mind playing tricks.

PEGGY Get off me! My skin crawls when you touch it! I could rip your lips off! *(She runs upstairs weeping)*

BOSLEY Peggy! Peggy!

PEGGY Am I living in hell? Is that it!? Have I gone straight to hell?!

In kitchen.

BOSLEY *(To Grizelda)* Don't leave this kitchen, Grizelda! I'm going to give Peggy her medication and I will be back to deal with you.

Peggy is sobbing in her room, putting on perfume. Bosley enters.

BOSLEY   Peg . . . ?

PEGGY   Get out!

BOSLEY   Let's have a little medication, all right? *(Takes out syringe)* You're just upset. Now, what's the matter? Everything was going so well. . . .

PEGGY   Get out of here, you stinking piece of flesh!

BOSLEY *(Advancing)*   Don't say those things, Peggy. Come on, this will make you feel better. Give me your arm. *(He touches her)*

PEGGY *(Jumps up, repulsed)*   YOU TOUCHED ME! OH GOD, MY FLESH IS ROTTING! THE TOUCH OF SCUM!

BOSLEY   Stop it, Peggy. Don't make me use force. Now, let me give you your shot or I'll have to call the hospital.

PEGGY   STAY AWAY!

She throws perfume in his face, blinding him.

BOSLEY *(Staggering)*   Oh God . . . Peggy, I'm going to have to commit you again! *(He drops syringe)*

PEGGY   Try it!

Peggy kicks him in the crotch and cracks him over the head with champagne bottle.

PEGGY   HELP! GRIZELDA, HELP ME! HE'S TRYING TO KILL ME! HELP!

Grizelda rushes up steps with broom.

Grizelda enters as Bosley comes to and tries to stand.

GRIZELDA BACK OFF, ASSHOLE! *(She hits him over the head with broom)* Are you all right, Mrs. Gravel? Did he hurt you?

PEGGY *(Hysterical)* No, but he tried! *(Bosley begins moving and Peggy starts screaming)* LOOK! LOOK! HE'S ATTACKING!

Grizelda rushes over, sits on his face, and slowly smothers him.

GRIZELDA Down, boy, down!

PEGGY *(Panicked)* He's dead, isn't he?

GRIZELDA (JEAN HILL): MURDER BY DERRIÈRE

GRIZELDA   We're in big trouble now, Miss Gravel!!

PEGGY *(Completely crazed)*   OH GOD, HE'S DEAD!

They both run from room screaming.

They run out of house, jump into Mercedes, and leave.

Grizelda and Peggy are fleeing the murder scene in Mercedes. They are out in the country.

PEGGY   Why did you bring me out here, Grizelda? To torture me? You know I hate nature! Look at these disgusting trees stealing my oxygen! *(Shot of car running over dead dog in the road)* I CAN'T STAND THIS SCENERY ANOTHER MINUTE! ALL NATURAL FORESTS SHOULD BE TURNED INTO HOUSING DEVELOPMENTS! I WANT CEMENT COVERING EVERY BLADE OF GRASS IN THIS NATION! DON'T WE TAXPAYERS HAVE A VOICE ANYMORE? . . .

GRIZELDA *(Suddenly losing patience)*   Do you ever shut up?! The police are looking for us, you know. We're gonna camp out here overnight.

PEGGY *(Terrified)*   CAMP OUT? NO, PLEASE, GRIZELDA! NOT THAT! I'LL DO ANYTHING YOU ASK BUT PLEASE NOT THAT!

Grizelda screeches on brakes, jumps out, and runs to Peggy's side and pulls her out by collar.

GRIZELDA   Now you listen to me, Mrs. Peggy Gravel!! You better calm yourself down before I haul off and smack you upside your wide, wide head! We killed your husband! I ain't your maid anymore, bitch! I am your SISTER IN CRIME!

PEGGY   Please . . . don't sit on me.

GRIZELDA *(Seeing Motorcycle Cop approach)*   Here come the honkers already!

Cop jumps from bike with gun drawn and begins to frisk them.

COP   Okay, witches! Up against the car!! Arms up on the roof! One false move and your heads will be flying through the trees!

GRIZELDA   What is this? Are you kidding me?

COP   Does it look like I'm kidding, Mau Mau?

PEGGY   Officer, I'm an outpatient from the hospital and I'm very prone to anxiety attacks, so please treat me with therapeutic courtesy.

COP   HA! I know who you are. There's an all-points bulletin out for both of you. You're Peggy Gravel and you killed your husband!

PEGGY   That's preposterous! We were about to have a picnic.

COP   Don't give me that shit—you were trying to escape to Mortville.

GRIZELDA   I never heard of no town called Mortville.

COP   Well, you should have, 'cause you belong there. It's a special town for people like you two; people who should be so embarrassed by what they done. I just might let you go there, that is, if you cooperate.

GRIZELDA   What do we have to do for you, Sheriff Shit-face?

COP   Sit up on that car hood, you'll see. *(His gums start to bleed)* I got something to show you first. *(He takes down pants to reveal complete woman's lingerie)* You like lingerie? I got some on I thought you might like to see. You like these little numbers? I sent away for 'em from Frederick's. They was expensive! *(Shot of Peggy and Grizelda in shocked disbelief) (Moaning)* OOOOOOHHHHHHH, I like the feel of that cold nylon on my big butt! OHHHHHHHH.

PEGGY   Will you please stop it! I have never found the antics of deviates to be one bit amusing.

COP *(To Grizelda)*   What I like best is a French kiss when I'm dressed.

GRIZELDA   Don't expect a kiss from me, liver lips!

COP   Take off your underpants! Come on, hand 'em over.

GRIZELDA   I knew cops were sick but . . . *(She takes them off and gives them to him)*

COP *(Aroused)*   Oh! These are big ones! A little plain for my taste but I think I'll slip them on . . . there! How does that look? Pretty sexy, huh? Now, how about that kiss?

GRIZELDA   If I kiss you, will you let us go?

COP *(Wagging his tongue obscenely)* You bet!!! *(He advances)* I want a wet one, now. *(They kiss passionately, he slobbers disgustingly)* OOOHHHH! *(He wipes his bleeding gums)* Goddamn gums! Yeah, that was a real soul kiss!

GRIZELDA *(Wiping her mouth)* Okay, buster, you had your fun. Now, which way to Mortville?

COP I ain't through yet. *(To Peggy)* Mrs. Gravel, I'd like to examine your underpants.

PEGGY I will not!

COP I thought you wanted to go to Mortville. They let . . . KILLERS live there, scot-free.

PEGGY *(Modestly takes them off)* I have never been so mortified in my entire life. *(Throws him her panties)* HERE, FLOTSAM!

COP *(He catches them in mouth)* That's more like it! MMMMMMMMMM. These are from Bloomingdale's, you got good taste. I think I'll try and fit my big business into 'em. *(Puts them on)* They're tight but they sure feel good!! *(Peggy and Grizelda look at each other in astonishment)* *(To Peggy)* Now do I get my little kiss-kiss?

PEGGY Please . . . I swear I'll gag. Mount me if you must, but please—not a kiss!

COP *(Advancing on Peggy)* Come on now . . . I'm all dressed up in my pretty underthings and I need a little lip suction. *(He kisses her repulsively)* *(Gums bleed)*

CROSS-DRESSING IN THE POLICE FORCE

AAAHHHHH I wish I could stick my whole head in your mouth and have you suck out my eyeballs! Would you like that? *(Panting)* I bet you would! *(Falling to ground, moaning and gurgling in climax)* *(Peggy and Grizelda watch in disgusted silence)* What are you hogs looking at? Go on— the show's over! Beat it! Mortville's up in the woods— follow the dirt road before I haul your ass to jail!!!

Peggy and Grizelda rush off.

Peggy and Grizelda struggle through wooded area in mist. They come to a clearing and we see Mortville, a hideous rural slum. Everything is made out of trash and garbage, including the houses. Hideous bums, perverts, and psychopaths walk the street as well-dressed "tourists" point and snap photos. Leather-clad Goons patrol the street harassing the pitiful citizens. In the distance we see a cheesy fairy-tale castle. Peggy and Grizelda walk through town, clutching on to each other in fear. They approach piewagon manned by cretinish Pieman.

GRIZELDA   I'll take a slice, please.

PIEMAN   Lemon meringue or chocolate?

GRIZELDA   Chocolate.

PIEMAN   That'll be ten cent.

GRIZELDA *(Paying him)*   Could you recommend a rooming house where we could spend the night? *(Pieman laughs*

WELCOME TO MORTVILLE

stupidly in her face) (Grizelda gives him a dirty look and moves)

PEGGY   I don't think I like it here. It's dirty and . . . the people are repulsive.

GRIZELDA   We don't have much choice, Peggy. It's better than jail.

PEGGY   I tell you, Grizelda, something's wrong here. Look around, it's a village of idiots! *(Shot of decrepit Mortville citizens)*

GRIZELDA   Can't you act normal!? Just act normal for a change!

They see "For Rent" sign in front of crummy house.

PEGGY   No, please! There must be a Quality Court or something! I can't go in that hogpen!

GRIZELDA   Oh, shut up. *(Rings bell)*

Mole McHenry answers the door. She is extremely masculine—bleached DA haircut and her face covered with moles and pimples. She is dressed in rags. She blows nose onto street by holding one nostril.

MOLE *(Rudely)*   Can I help you?

PEGGY   We've been raped, please give us shelter!

MOLE   *You* were raped?

GRIZELDA   Don't pay no attention to her—look, we need to rent a room.

A NEW HOME

MOLE   You got money on you?

PEGGY   I am a very wealthy woman.

MOLE   Yeah? And I'm Cybill Shepherd. Come on in here—
we might work something out. That is, IF you got money.

They walk into atrocious, poverty-stricken living room.

MOLE   My name's Mole. Mole McHenry.

PEGGY   I'm Peggy Gravel. It's nice to meet you.

Mole gives her a dirty look and spits.

GRIZELDA   I'm Grizelda, Grizelda Brown. I'm Peggy's . . .
psychiatric nurse.

MOLE   The room's out back, nothing fancy but it's a roof
over your head. Come on, I'll show you. *(They exit)*

*They walk through seedy bedroom. Someone is in the bed,
under covers.*

MOLE   Shhh! My girl friend's sleeping.

They walk across back lawn to hideous shack.

MOLE   You're lucky it's empty. My last tenant shot himself
in here last night. The dumb fuck left a mess everywhere!

*They walk into shack. Bed is unmade with stained sheets
and the corpse of old bum lies on bed.*

MOLE   Damn, it stinks in here! Well, what d'you think? You
want it or not?

GRIZELDA *(Holding her nose, gagging)* Will . . . *he* be removed?

MOLE Yeah, I'll get the stiff outa here but don't think I have time for *all* the chores in the world. *(Picking up blood-stained sheets)* And no linens until I soak these in cold water . . . and we don't have no toilets in Mortville.

PEGGY Well, how do we . . . ?

MOLE I guess you'll just have to use your imagination.

PEGGY I see . . . I see.

MOLE *(To Grizelda)* How much cash you got?

GRIZELDA *(Looking in bag)* Well . . . I . . .

MOLE *(Snatching her bag)* Gimme that! *(Going through wallet)* Six bucks!! *(Excited)* Hey, you are a rich one . . . *a lottery ticket!!!* I'll take that too and I'll win it! . . . What's this? A bankbook. *(Throws it down)* A lot of good that'll do you here!

PEGGY *(Panicked)* There . . . there aren't any banks in Mortville?

MOLE There ain't nothing here, lady! Nobody's got one red cent in Mortville except for that queen!!!

GRIZELDA The Queen? Could she help us?

MOLE You got a lot to learn about living in Mortville.

GRIZELDA We'd like to take the room.

MOLE   It's all yours, sweetheart. You hungry? I'm going to eat myself some chow and I got a little extra. Looks like you got a big appetite.

PEGGY   I'd be happy to help with the preparation.

MOLE *(Disgustedly)*   Oh, this one takes the cake!

They enter Mole's living room.

MOLE   You both sure are ugly bitches. Go on, sit down. *(Yelling offscreen)* Hey, Muffy, we got company. *(She throws crummy plates and broken plastic forks down on table)*

PEGGY   We really hadn't planned on coming here. We're from the Guilford neighborhood in Baltimore.

MOLE   I been to Baltimore a few times. Bumberg! I hate it, all them hillbilly fucks lookin' at you.

GRIZELDA   If you want the truth, we had no choice but to come to Mortville.

PEGGY   We're in a lot of trouble. You see, I'm quite prominent and we . . . accidentally killed my husband.

MOLE   Hey, I don't care what you did! Nobody's in Mortville for a vacation. We all did something or we wouldn't be here in the first place. *(Takes out a raw possum)* Dinner's served!

PEGGY *(Appalled)*   I'm really not that hungry.

MOLE *(Riled up)*   I invited you to dinner and you accepted!! You'll eat this if I have to jam it down your throat! *(Starts carving it) (Handing Grizelda a portion)* HEY MUFFY, I CALLED you to DINNER! Do I have to come in there and smack you?!! *(Hands Peggy a serving)*

Muffy St. Jacques enters, still half asleep. She is an exaggerated blond glamour-girl type, va-va-voom figure, dressed in skimpy, see-through curtains she has pieced together for clothes.

MUFFY   You don't have to shout the house down—I heard you all right already.

MOLE   This is my girl friend, Muffy St. Jacques. The most beautiful woman in all of Mortville.

MUFFY   Hi. *(She rubs breasts suggestively in Peggy's face)*

MOLE   This is Grizelda. . . . *(To Peggy)* And I forget your name.

PEGGY   Peggy. Peggy Gravel. It's a pleasure. We rent the room out back so I guess we'll be neighbors.

MUFFY   Oh really? I sleep in that room right near you— NAKED!!

MOLE   You're five minutes late for dinner, Muffy. Don't you remember our little talk about your laziness?

MUFFY   I was having an erotic dream.

MOLE   I warned you about thinking about men before your afternoon nap! Dirty thoughts about dirty men bring on dirty dreams and you're a dirty girl, Muffy!

PINK FLAMINGOS AND OTHER FILTH

MUFFY   I can't help what I think about, Mole. It's not my fault Mr. Sandman's not a bulldozer like you.

MOLE   I'm warning you, Muffy.

MUFFY   Oh, Mole, sometimes I need a man.

MOLE   I'm a man, Muffy. A man trapped in a woman's body.

MUFFY   Oh, but Mole, you don't have that same big deal.

She reaches for food and Mole spears her hand with carving fork.

MOLE   Take it back!!

MUFFY   Oh God, Mole, it hurts! Take it out!

MOLE   Take back what you said to me!

MUFFY   I'm sorry, Mole. You're the only one! I love you, my man, I'm only queer for you, Mole!

Mole takes fork out, Muffy rubs hand.

MOLE   That's better, Muffy. *(To guests)* Muffy knows how I feel about men; I'm not one to be pushed over my limit.

MUFFY   That hurt.

Two Mortville Goons bust in door.

GOON 1 *(To Peggy and Grizelda)* There they are! Don't move, scags.

GOON 2 You both are under arrest by the order of Her Majesty Queen Carlotta. Anything you say could put you in front of the firing squad!!

GRIZELDA Take it easy. We're not fightin' you.

PEGGY *(Hysterical, weeping)* Help us! Please help us!

MOLE Don't worry. It's standard procedure in Mortville.

MUFFY Can I get you a cup of gin or anything, officer?

GOON 1 Stay back, peasant woman! *(He hustles Peggy and Grizelda out the door)*

≋≋≋

Inside paddy wagon. It is a dark, bumpy ride. Peggy breaks down sobbing as Grizelda comforts her. Grizelda kisses her lightly. Peggy responds but then her eyes open wide in disbelief at what is happening.

PEGGY Oh, Grizelda, I can't.

GRIZELDA Peggy! Peggy!

Paddy wagon stops in front of Queen Carlotta's fairy-tale castle. Drawbridge comes down and Peggy and Grizelda are dragged inside. SS-type soldiers hang out in hallway making obscene gestures and trying to maul prisoners as they are led by. In background we see framed portraits of Idi Amin, Hitler, and Manson.

Peggy and Grizelda are dragged into throne room over to custom-built kneelers built with restraints.

Peggy and Grizelda are weeping, terrified.

GOON 2   That's where they all belong! Down on their knees!

GOON 1 *(Chaining them) (In mock baby voices)*   Don't be crying, CRYBABY! DADDY'S NOT GOING TO LEAVE YOU!

A royal page enters and blows trumpet.

GOON 3   Her Majesty, The Honorable Queen Carlotta of Mortville.

Queen Carlotta enters, being carried by Goons on platform. She is in her sixties, overweight, has very few teeth, and wears a perpetual sneer. She struggles into her elaborate throne.

QUEEN   Welcome to Mortville, ladies! I read in the big-city papers that you are wanted for murder; the murder of a certain Mr. Bosley Gravel.

PEGGY   We only . . .

QUEEN *(Furious)*   YOU ARE INTERRUPTING MY FLOW OF POWER! GIVE THESE PEASANTS A LITTLE DINNER, LIEUTENANT WILSON! I BET THEY'RE HUNGRY AFTER A LONG DAY OF BREAKING LAWS!

Wilson brings out platter of roaches and forces them down their throats.

WILSON   Eat these goddamn roaches!

PINK FLAMINGOS AND OTHER FILTH

THE GOONS

QUEEN CARLOTTA (EDITH MASSEY)

QUEEN Now listen to me, riffraff! Every word I ever utter is to be taken as a direct royal proclamation! . . . OR FACE DEATH BY THE FIRING SQUAD!

GRIZELDA *(Petrified)* Yes . . . ma'am.

QUEEN MA'AM?! I am Your Royal Highness and I demand you address me as such!

GRIZELDA Yes . . . Your Royal Highness.

QUEEN *(Smiles)* Let's show them we're not kidding, Lieutenant Wilson. Bring in the prisoner.

Wilson brings in Eater, a horrid biker type.

QUEEN Any last words, goon face?

EATER You can lick my royal hemorrhoids, you fat pig!

QUEEN Oh, ready, aim, fire.

Eater is shot by Goons.

QUEEN *(To a stunned Peggy and Grizelda)* I advise you to listen carefully, rubbish! Royal proclamation number one: *(Trumpet sounds)* As long as you live in Mortville, I must always be considered your God! If you should ever see me on the streets, fall to your knees and shout, "I honor you, Queen Carlotta!" Royal proclamation number two: *(Trumpet sounds)* You must live here in constant mortification, solely existing to bring me and my tourists a few moments of royal amusement. I am not responsible for your income, living conditions, or personal happiness. Have I made myself perfectly clear?

GRIZELDA   Yes . . . Your Royal Majesty.

QUEEN   And you . . . Mrs. Gravel, murderess?

PEGGY   You've made yourself quite clear.

QUEEN   Your . . . ?

PEGGY   Your Royal Majesty.

QUEEN   So be it. Lieutenant Williams, take them to our ugly experts and give them a complete overhaul. *(To Peggy and Grizelda)* When you walk down the streets of Mortville, make sure you dress like what you are. TRASH! *(To Lieutenant)* REMOVE THEM! *(They are dragged out)* *(Relaxing)* Ah, are my duties of discipline ever over? Remove me from this contraption, Lieutenant Wilson.

WILSON *(Genuflecting)*   I honor you, Queen Carlotta.

QUEEN   Oh, yes . . . I know, I know. Just get me into my royal cot and be quick.

A royal cot is wheeled in and she is placed in it. Cot has horn.

WILLIAMS   If it pleases the Queen, Royal Security has reported that Princess Coo-Coo has returned to the castle. She's been out all night again . . . *(Coughs)* with that garbageman!

QUEEN *(Pained)*   Oh, that child'll be the death of me yet. Take me to her chambers.

EATER AND LIEUTENANT WILSON (KENNY ORYE AND ED PERANIO)

PRINCESS COO-COO (MARY VIVIAN PEARCE)

Queen is wheeled down hall, honking at Goons in the way, who genuflect. They wheel her to Princess's chamber.

Ridiculously frilly bedroom. Princess Coo-Coo, in her royal drag, sits on bed reading a love comic book. She wears her hair in Shirley Temple curls and her face is a grotesque mass of makeup. She looks like a young Baby Jane.

QUEEN *(Barging in)* I'll call you when I need you, Lieutenant Williams. Coo-Coo, I must have a little talk with you.

COO-COO Oh, leave me alone, Mummy, I've had a wonderful evening and I don't want it spoiled with your nosy nagging.

QUEEN   A wonderful evening? . . . With a garbageman?!

COO-COO   He's not a garbageman . . . he just helps pick up trash at the nudist colony.

QUEEN   I hardly think a nudist janitor is a proper escort for a royal princess!

COO-COO   I'm thirty-eight years old and I can date who I please. You've got no right to order me around like one of your subjects!

QUEEN   You may not realize it, Coo-Coo, but you have an awesome responsibility on your shoulders. One day all of Mortville will be yours and you must learn to rule with dignity.

COO-COO *(Throwing crown down—Queen is shocked)*   I'm not going to be queen of anywhere! I want to marry Herbert.

QUEEN   Herbert!!? Is that his name!?

COO-COO   It's a beautiful name!

QUEEN   You'd step down from the throne for the love of a mutant?

COO-COO   Oh, Mummy, I love him.

QUEEN   Well, I won't have it! I'm afraid I'm going to have to punish you, Coo-Coo. You are forbidden to leave your room until your fortieth birthday!

COO-COO *(Having a fit)*   I won't stay in this castle! I love Herbert and I'm going to marry him and you won't stop me! *(Nose starts bleeding)* Now you've given me another nosebleed! I hate this stupid town! *(Weeping with nosebleed, throwing her head back)* Get out of here. Leave me in peace!

Lieutenant Wilson enters.

WILSON *(Checking for trouble)* Excuse me, Your Highness. . . .

QUEEN Take me to my bedroom and lock Coo-Coo in for the night.

COO-COO *(Stomping her feet, crying)* NO! NO! NO!

Queen is wheeled out and door is locked.

QUEEN That daughter of mine is a delinquent. I'm going to have to take drastic steps with her.

Queen Carlotta's royal bedroom. She is wheeled in and struggles toward bed.

WILSON Can you make it, Your Majesty?

QUEEN I suppose.

Wilson shoves her onto bed.

QUEEN *(Flirting)* I believe it's your night to service me, Lieutenant Wilson.

WILSON *(Stripping)* I am always eager, Your Highness. *(He gets into bed)*

QUEEN   Whip it out and show it hard. Come on, daddy, fuck me! Ooh, glow little inchworm! Look at that pelt! Look at those balls!

Wilson starts to kiss her.

QUEEN   Don't bother with the head! The V of my crotch is what needs attention! *(He mounts her)*

WILSON   I can fuck like a bandit, Your Highness.

QUEEN   Well, rob my safety-deposit box, then. Dig for gold, baby. Dig for gold!

WILSON   Oh . . . Your Highness. I'm entering the royal tunnel!

QUEEN   Go, daddy. Go all night. Get it, get it, get it!

Mole's living room.

Grizelda and Peggy enter, done up in the new Mortville style forced on them by the "ugly expert." Peggy has dyed black hair and tacky outfit. Grizelda has gone blond and wears a ridiculous sequined tutu.

Mole and Muffy jump up.

MOLE *(To Peggy)*   Pretty outfits.

Mole and Muffy start laughing at their foolish clothes.

PEGGY *(Angry)*   Funny, is it!? Well, let me tell you I wouldn't wear this outfit to a dogfight! You two may have

A NEW FASHION LOOK

resigned yourselves to a subhuman life in this slum of a town, but I, Peggy Gravel, have not!

MUFFY   You better hush up before Mole loses her temper and smacks you.

GRIZELDA   Just shut up, Peggy.

PEGGY   No I won't shut up! You shut up! I'll tell you—my blue blood is about ready to boil!

MOLE   Hey, you listen to me, wacko! See this fist? I'm about ready to use that hatchet face of yours as a punching bag! Now sit down and shut up!

GRIZELDA   Mole's right, Peggy. I'm sick of listening to your bitching! Next time you feel a fit coming on, go outside and bitch. Bitch at the trees, bitch at the air, but don't bitch at us!

PEGGY *(Weakly)* My bitching isn't relieved if there's no one to hear it.

MUFFY Well, we can't all be your psychiatrist, honey. We got problems of our own.

PEGGY Why . . . why are you in Mortville?

MUFFY Oh, it's a long, ugly story.

MOLE Tell her, Muffy, maybe she'd stop feeling sorry for herself.

MUFFY I didn't always used to be like this. I mean, I've always been visually stunning but . . . I used to be married and I had a baby named Freddie. It was about three years ago and my husband and I were returning from a cocktail party . . .

Flashback.

Interior car. Muffy, looking younger and more suburban, is fuming next to her square Husband, who is drunk behind the wheel.

MUFFY Let me drive!

HUSBAND Get off! I can drive! Always trying to boss me around!

MUFFY You're drunk, per usual. Every time we step out of the house you get dead drunk!

HUSBAND   When you're married to a nag, a man's gotta drink.

MUFFY   First I have to be mortified in front of our friends, now I have to be mortified in front of the baby-sitter. I suppose *I'll* have to drive her home.

HUSBAND   I'll take her! *(Swerving)*

MUFFY *(Grabbing wheel)*   You'll take her all right! Straight to the graveyard! NOW LET ME DRIVE!

HUSBAND   GET OFF!

They pull up in front of their suburban home. The baby-sitter is having a wild party. Kids are drunk on the lawn and the house is all lit up. Muffy and Husband rush in. Kids panic, jump through windows, knock over furniture. Muffy runs past drunk who has passed out after vomiting on picture of Husband.

MUFFY *(Trying to find her baby)*   Freddie!! Freddie!! Oh, God, my little Freddie!!

Husband sees his liquor gone, starts fighting with kids. Falls down drunkenly.

HUSBAND   Get off my liquor, you little punk!

MUFFY *(Runs up steps, knocking kids out of the way, into nursery. Baby's crib is empty)*   FREDDIE! OH GOD, FREDDIE!! *(Runs into master bedroom. Sitter is half nude on a bad trip in Muffy's bed, making love with hippie jerk. Muffy's clothes are thrown all over the room)*

MUFFY *(Smacking her)*   Linda! Where's Freddie?

LINDA   I don't know, I'm tripping!

MUFFY *(Shaking her)*   Where is my baby?!!

LINDA   I think I put him in the kitchen.

Muffy runs down steps and into kitchen frantically search-ing for baby. She hesitates, opens refrigerator door, and we see screaming baby inside. Muffy snatches him out, hugging him, trying to comfort his hysterical tears. Linda enters, hallucinating.

LINDA   Hey, you got any downers?

MUFFY *(Shaking her)*   You filthy tramp! My baby was in the refrigerator!!

LINDA   So don't pay me! Don't pay me!

MUFFY *(Outraged)*   PAY YOU? WHY, YOU LITTLE SNIP!

Muffy hits Linda over head with frying pan and then forces her semiconscious face into big bowl of dog food on floor, painfully smothering her.

Husband enters and tries to pull Muffy off victim.

HUSBAND   Are you crazy? Are you trying to kill her!?

MUFFY *(Shoves him)*   You drunken sot! *(Screaming uncon-trollably, totally flipped out)* GET YOUR STINKING LI-QUOR BREATH OUT OF MY FACE!!!

Muffy runs to car and tries to flee. Husband tries to lean in car to grab her and she puts power window up on his neck and drives off, dragging a kicking and screaming torso behind her.

Flashback dissolves.

Return to scene.

Grizelda and Peggy are in awe.

MUFFY *(Softly crying)* I've never seen my baby again. The press still calls me the "dog-food murderess." I can never go back. I couldn't bear the shame.

GRIZELDA And you, Mole? . . . What happened to you?

MOLE I been in Mortville for ten long years and I tell ya— it isn't very pretty what a town without pity can do. What brought me here was a championship wrestlin' match. It was back in 1966, and I was fightin' under the name of Wrasslin' Rita. My challenger was Big Jimmy Dong, the Human Blockhead.

Flashback.

Wrasslin' Rita is dressed in leopard-print wrestling outfit with obscene vagina sculpted on front.

Wrasslin' Rita rushes out and fans throw beer cans.

Fight. Wrasslin' Rita flips him around, screeching grotesquely. Wrasslin' Rita finally kicks him in balls and attacks with high heel, gouging out his eye. She then stomps on his eyeball. She goes wild and attacks referee with mike cord and strangles him.

Flashback dissolves.

WRASSLIN' RITA (SUSAN LOWE)

THE END OF A CAREER

MOLE   That ended my professional wrasslin' career and I've been here ever since, sitting in my own stink and trying to figure a way out. But our luck's gonna be changin', right, Muff?

MUFFY *(Beaming)*   Right, Mole! We're going to win that lottery!

PEGGY   I believe that was *our* lottery ticket!

MOLE *(Jumping up)*   It WAS yours. But you rented a room, asswipe, and that ticket's mine now.

PEGGY *(Going nuts)*   You better give me my share! We need money. We're not trash like you! We're not used to this low-class life!

MOLE   I'll wipe the floor up with you! *(They start struggling)*

MUFFY   Kill her, Mole! Break her arms! Rip her hair out!

GRIZELDA *(Butting in)*   Break it up. *(Getting Peggy in head-lock) (They stop)* Now, stop it, you two! Those lottery tickets aren't any good anyway! The odds are a million to one!

MUFFY   Don't say that! You'll hex our good luck!

MOLE   I'm warnin' you both! You better stay out of my way, because when ole Mole gets mean, there's no telling what she'll do.

GRIZELDA   Peggy, I think it's time for bed now. We both need a good night's sleep.

PEGGY   I'll sleep all right! Maybe in my dreams I can forget this rotten little town and its disgusting population! As far as I'm concerned, you two *BELONG* in Mortville.

≋≋≋

Fade to shot of moon with dogs howling in background.

Shot of Grizelda and Peggy asleep on single cot. Grizelda is completely nude except for pair of high-top tennis shoes. Grizelda rolls over on top of a terrified Peggy and begins mauling her.

Intercut with Muffy and Mole wildly making love.

Grizelda starts moaning and forcing Peggy down on her. Peggy gives in and we see her head disappear offscreen.

PEGGY   If it's good enough for Gertrude Stein . . .

GRIZELDA   Get it! Get it! Get it!

Grizelda moans in ecstasy. Fade out.

≋≋≋

Fade in to shot of sunrise in Mortville.

Shot of Muffy and Mole asleep. Roaches crawl over Muffy's ass.

Shot of Mortville Goons banging on doors and yelling through loudspeaker.

GOON A   Wake up, you pitiful creatures!

GOON B   Get your fat asses outa the sack! First busload of tourists about to enter!

Shot of Mole going to door.

GUARD *(Nailing proclamations)* Royal proclamation! All residents must read the royal proclamation. *(Puts one on Mole's door) (Mole comes to door)* Here, stupid. Hahaha-hahahaha!

She reads it and storms into bedroom. Muffy is getting up.

MOLE   You won't believe this, Muffy!

MUFFY   What now?

MOLE   That cow has gone too far this time! Listen to this shit: "Royal Proclamation—Queen Carlotta has declared today as Backwards Day. All residents must wear their clothes backwards and walk backwards at all times. Anyone who fails to perform for the tourists will be immediately executed!"

MUFFY   Ah, God. You mean we have to walk around backwards all day?

MOLE   It looks that way, Muffy.

MUFFY   On an empty stomach yet. I'm starvin' to death, Mole.

MOLE *(Enters kitchen)* The cupboard's bare, Muffy. It ain't right to wake up hearing your own stomach growling. *(Growling)*

MUFFY *(Entering)* We'll have to wait until the food dump, I guess.

MOLE *(Searching for food)* Everywhere I look's a big nothing! I'd eat anything.

MUFFY I know, Mole. I'm so hungry I could eat cancer!

A cat comes in door with a dead rat in his mouth.

MOLE Well, isn't this a godsend! *(Takes rat from his mouth)* Pussy brought daddy some breakfast? *(Throws it in pan, spits for grease, and lights rubbish fire to cook it)* I hope those other two aren't expecting a Continental breakfast, 'cause old Mole's gonna chomp this down in one big bite! *(She begins to cook it)*

Cut to shot of big junk-food breakfast. Queen Carlotta is in her bed, packing it away. Zoom back to reveal whole bed filled with huge junk-food breakfast. Bird lands on window.

QUEEN Well, good morning, little birdie! You're a cute little fellow. Want some pizza? *(Feeds him)* Hungry, huh? Yes. Birdie, birdie, birdie. I bet you flew all the way to Mortville just to see Backwards Day, didn't you? Well, you flew to the right window, 'cause I am your queen! *(Bird chirps)*

Lieutenant Wilson barges in.

WILSON Excuse me, Your Majesty, but Princess Coo-Coo has escaped from her royal bedroom.

QUEEN *(Alarmed)* She WHAT?! That little M.F.! *(Trying to get out of bed)* Come on! Get me into my cot!

WILSON *(Blows whistle to signal—other soldiers run in)* I honor you, Your Majesty!

They lift her to cot and wheel her out. Queen honks horn impatiently as they go down hall.

Queen is rolled into Coo-Coo's bedroom. Window is open with sheets knotted together and hanging down.

On the mirror, written in lipstick: "Fuck you, Mummy."

QUEEN *(Reading note, pissed)* That ungrateful little whippersnapper!

WILSON She escaped by shinnying down this rope of sheets.

QUEEN On Backwards Day, yet! I want you morons to find her! And as for that garbageman, I want him shot on sight! *(Going nuts)* Damn that little hellcat of a daughter! That good-for-nothing, simple-minded scalawag! Damn! Damn! *Dammit!*

Mole and Muffy enter street.

They see everyone walking backwards. They realize it's Backwards Day and moan, and enter onto the street backwards.

The next-door neighbor, Mr. Paul, a bum drag queen, is sweeping his porch backwards.

MUFFY Hi, Mr. Paul.

MR. PAUL   Hi, dollface. This Backwards Day is a lot of shit, ain't it?

MOLE   It sure is, Mr. Paul. It sure is.

Mr. Paul starts laughing hysterically.

Peggy and Grizelda enter backwards. Mole and Muffy snub them and walk away, backwards.

They all walk backwards to nudist camp. Peggy and Grizelda follow.

Shot of Mortville nudists playing volleyball on pogo sticks. It is obviously cold outside.

Shot of Herbert, nudist garbageman, picking up trash.

Muffy knocks on nudist-camp entrance. Mole, Peggy, and Grizelda are behind her.

Shina, the head nudist, goes to answer.

SHINA   Sorry! Nudists only! No tourists.

MUFFY   It's me, Muffy!

Shina opens door.

SHINA   Well, why didn't you say it was the most beautiful woman in Mortville? *(Muffy hugs her and they enter)*

MOLE   Hi, Shina.

SHINA   Hey, Mr. Mole.

MUFFY   This is Peggy and Grizelda. They're new in Mortville.

SHINA *(Shakes hands)*   It's nice to meet you.

MOLE   Hey, Shina, you got a newspaper around? We wanna
see if we won the Maryland lottery.

HERBERT, THE NUDIST GARBAGEMAN (GEORGE FIGGS)

SHINA   Oh, Mole, you know newspapers are contraband. *(Whispering)* But I sure hope you do win. This town could stand a little glamour! I tell you I'm getting fed up!

MOLE   We're all fed up, Shina. At least you don't have to participate in Backwards Day.

SHINA   I know . . . I'm surprised the Queen didn't order me to wear my vagina backwards! *(They all laugh)*

Princess Coo-Coo rushes in.

They all fall to knees.

COO-COO   Excuse me, but I must see Herbert—Herbert my love.

ALL   I honor you, Princess Coo-Coo.

COO-COO   Oh, stop it!! You don't have to do that! I'm not like my mother, I'm a normal person! Come on now, get up! Get up! *(They do)*

SHINA   Herbert's out there picking up garbage as usual, Princess Coo-Coo, but please, if you two are having an affair, you better be careful. That Queen will cut off your ears!

COO-COO   Let her do it, then! Herbert doesn't care if I have ears, he only cares about my mind! *(She rushes out)*

Princess runs in slow motion toward Herbert. Herbert sees her, drops his stick, and rushes to her.

COO-COO   Herbert! Herbert!

HERBERT   Coo-Coo! Coo-Coo!

They kiss passionately.

Nudists are touched. So are Mole et al.

HERBERT *(Kissing her)* Oh, Coo, I worship the ground you walk on! I couldn't keep my mind on my work all morning —every piece of trash I had to pick up reminded me of you. An old candy wrapper made me think of how sweet you are, a snotty Kleenex made me realize how much I'd

IN BETWEEN TAKES AT THE NUDIST CAMP
(PAT MORAN, MY ASSISTANT, AND MARY VIVIAN PEARCE)

cry if we ever parted, and an old rubber made me think of all the nights of eros we have before us. I love you, Coo-Coo.

COO-COO   Oh, Herbert, I masturbated fourteen times last night just thinking about you, and when I finally did fall asleep my dreams were not exactly dry! Take me now, Herbert, right in front of the whole town! Take me, Herbert, take me!!!

Just as Herbert starts to make love to her, we see Mortville Goons with guns drawn. They shoot him, and he falls dead on top of Princess.

COO-COO *(Flipping out, trying to get up)*   No! No! No! Oh God no!! Herbert! Herbert! Oh, my baby darling Herbert!

Peggy, Grizelda, Mole, and Muffy rush out of nudist camp backwards.

PEGGY *(Weeping)*   Where are we going, Grizelda? What hell lays in store for us now?!

GRIZELDA   I don't know, Peggy, just keep up with Mole.

They approach Flipper's Bar. Drunken monstrosities hang out in beer garden, vomiting, cursing, laughing.

They enter bar and take a seat. Chris, the barmaid, waves.

Inside bar various scary women loiter, guzzling. It is a derelict lesbian bar. On a raised platform is Flipper, wildly dancing, guzzling. She has a Thalidomide stub arm and part of her act is kicking and taunting a man tied up.

Flipper winks to Mole and Muffy in recognition.

PEGGY *(Scared)* What kind of bar is this?

MOLE Who asked you to sit with us anyway?

Shot of Flipper whipping man.

Audience is turned on.

PEGGY *(Appalled)* I . . . I have to use the ladies' room.

MOLE The pisshole's out back.

GRIZELDA I'll save your seat, lover.

Peggy uneasily walks through bar, through dark orgy room, where women grab her, out back to public rest room.

Peggy enters washroom. Woman pervert tries to grab her under stall. They struggle.

Peggy is on toilet and two giant breasts come through twin glory holes.

Peggy screams and runs out, fighting off bathroom pervert.

PEGGY No! Please! Leave me alone! *(She rushes back into bar)*

We see her struggling to get out of orgy room. Another woman pervert is being dragged along by teeth as she holds on to Peggy's leg brace.

Flipper is still dancing lewdly, kicking man.

FLIPPER (COOKIE MUELLER)

MUFFY *(To Peggy)*   Wild, isn't it??

PEGGY   I'm really not trying to be rude but I can't stay here any longer.

MOLE   What's the matter, don't you like fun?

PEGGY   This is NOT my idea of fun! Grizelda, please walk me back to the house.

GRIZELDA *(Drinking)*   Oh, loosen up a bit!

PEGGY   I have no desire to be a loose person! And stop drinking, before you get dead drunk!

GRIZELDA *(Sighing)*   Come on, I'll walk you back.

MUFFY   Hey, Peggy, I don't get you!

MOLE   You leech onto us, and then all you can do is complain.

MUFFY   Let the little babies go home! If you don't like this bar, there's *really* something the matter with you!

Peggy and Grizelda exit.

Flipper mocks killing of man by hitting him over the head with steel ball on chain. All applaud wildly, including Muffy and Mole.

Mole, Muffy, and Flipper approach Flipper's car-house.

A midget exits from car, tucking in shirttail and arranging her hair.

FLIPPER *(Yanking open car door to reveal Shotsie in seminudity with food, liquor, and trash all over car)* You lazy bitch! I'm out workin' my tail off all day and you're home fucking midgets! Isn't that the pits!

SHOTSIE Ah, Flipper, don't start that shit! She's just an old friend of mine. Come on, get in here!

FLIPPER Friend my ass! You've turned my apartment into your own private passion pit, haven't you?

SHOTSIE Cram it, Flipper. Not in front of company.

MOLE *(Embarrassed)* Sorry if we interrupted anything.

SHOTSIE You didn't interrupt nothing, Mole. Flipper's so jealous she thinks the toilet I sit on is her competition. What can I do for you? *(Flipper sulks)*

MOLE We're trying to find today's paper.

SHOTSIE Yeah, I got one around here somewhere. Here you go.

Muffy and Mole rip open paper for lottery listings.

Shotsie grabs Flipper and kisses her. Flipper gives in.

MUFFY *(Excitedly)* There it is—Maryland lottery listings! *(Crosses her fingers)*

MOLE 0-8555-321 *(Checking her ticket)* I told you! We did it, Muffy! We qualify for the finalist drawing!!! Oh shit, we won a thousand dollars. We're rich, we're rich!

MUFFY *(Jumping up and down)* At last I got a sugar daddy!!! Oh Mole! Oh thank you, lady luck! Thank you! *(They embrace)*

Shot of Queen being carried down the street on raised platform by her soldiers. Townspeople fall to knees shouting, "We honor you, Queen Carlotta."

QUEEN *(Laughing and pointing to citizens on Backwards Day)* Hey, moron, you got your clothes on backwards! Hahahahaha! Oh God, this is fun!! Hi, stupid! Hi, ugly!

Mole, Muffy, Flipper, and Shotsie are at attention but angry.

SHOTSIE That senile old cunt.

MOLE I wish I had a rifle with a telescopic lens on it!

FLIPPER I'd help you pull the trigger, Mole.

MUFFY Squeaky Fromme, where are you when we need you?

MOLE *(Rolling a mudball)* I can't resist! That hog face is too much of a moving target to ignore. *(Throws mudball and hits Queen)*

Queen is furious, scanning the crowd, looking for assailant.

QUEEN God damn it! Who threw that?!

Fade to Princess Coo-Coo with Herbert's corpse inside Peggy and Grizelda's cottage.

DESPERATE LIVING

FLIPPER, SHOTSIE (SHARON NIESP), MOLE, AND
MUFFY GET READY TO ATTACK

COO-COO *(Insanely talking to corpse)* Oh Herbert, we're safe now. I'm sorry I had to drag you all that way, but those silly nudists wanted to BURY you! *(Kisses him)* Oh I love you too, my darling—Mother can't hurt us now. We'll get married tonight. *(Kisses him and cuddles)* You don't look so well, I hope you perk up for our honeymoon!

Enter Grizelda and Peggy. They are shocked.

PEGGY   What the hell is this?

COO-COO *(Jumping up)* Oh, I'm sorry, I know it's rude to bring my lover to your home, especially since I don't even know you, but my mother's army is trying to kill my Herbert. . . .

PEGGY   Young woman, that man is already dead!

COO-COO *(Rushing to him)*   No, he's not! He's just sleeping. *(Cuddling up next to him)* Aren't you, Herbert? Say hi to the nice ladies.

GRIZELDA   You better get your lily-white ass outa here before we *all* get shot.

COO-COO   Please don't kick me out!! Those soldiers are lookin' for me, and my mother will lock me up in that castle if she finds me.

PEGGY   You obviously belong in a mental hospital!

GRIZELDA   Look who's calling the kettle black. She's just upset, now be easy with her.

PEGGY   I will not! I don't want some renegade necrophile princess as *my* roommate!

GRIZELDA   It's just for a few days. Don't be so selfish!

PEGGY   Selfish!!! I'll show you selfish!! *(To Princess, pulling her)* Get out of here, mongrel, and take your stinkin' corpse of a boyfriend with you! *(Kicks her in ass)*

COO-COO *(Collapsing next to Herbert, kissing him)*   Oh, Herbert, this lady's being so mean to me.

GRIZELDA *(Putting her arm around Princess, trying to comfort her)*   Don't cry Princess, I'll try and help you some way.

PEGGY   Why don't you just kiss her and get it over with!? Huh, Grizelda?

GRIZELDA *(Gives Peggy a dirty look)* *(To Coo-Coo, arm around her)*   There, there. Everything'll be all right.

PEGGY   Go ahead, feel her up! Just like you did to me! Find 'em, feel 'em, fuck 'em, forget 'em—I guess that's your new motto?!!!

GRIZELDA *(Getting angry)*   Zip that gaping hole of a mouth, Peggy, before I plug it up with my fist!

PEGGY   You're just like all the rest of the common dykes in this town! *(Runs to door)*

GRIZELDA *(Leaping at Peggy)*   Dyke? What do you mean dyke?

PEGGY *(Opening door to yell)*   Help! Police! The Princess is in my house!

Goons come running to Peggy's rescue and whisk her away. Inside Grizelda overpowers the first Goon and

JEAN HILL POSES BEFORE HER DEATH SCENE

shoots him with his own gun. Another Goon enters and Grizelda strangles him. Coo-Coo hides under the bed with Herbert's corpse. Another Goon enters and Grizelda throws him right through the wall of the house. The whole house teeters and collapses on Grizelda.

Shot of Grizelda mortally wounded by falling two-by-four with sharp nail that pierces her head.

Injured Goons drag the hysterical Coo-Coo from the rubble.

GOON   Come on, bitch, your mother wants to see you!

COO-COO *(Sobbing)*   Herbert! Herbert!

Shot of Mole and Muffy entering their house later.

MOLE   I knew I shoulda gotten a security deposit from those assholes!

MUFFY   Yeah, you let riffraff move in and they bring the neighborhood down every time!

MOLE   Look, I gotta get my ass into Baltimore to claim our money and do some shopping. Will you be all right while I'm gone?

MUFFY   I'll be all right. Just you be careful.

MOLE   Lock those doors and don't fuck any men! *(She exits)*

Cut to half-naked soldier, Lieutenant Grogan, wildly bumping and grinding as the Queen watches, leering and moaning.

QUEEN *(Applauding, wildly aroused)* Ch-ch-ch-ch-ch-ch! Take it off! Come on, let's see some ass! *(Grogan shakes his ass at her)* Yeah! Yeah! Strip faster! Let's see some private areas! *(He strips to jockstrap)* Ohhhh I see London, I see France!! Spread those legs, baby! I want meat and potatoes! Yeahhhh! A Hollywood loaf!!! *(Soldier throws Queen his jockstrap, she caresses it)* Yessssirrreee! Come on over here with that thing! *(He approaches)* You're a wicked little boy getting me all heated up, aren't you?!! I'm going to have to give you a spanking!!

GROGAN I've been a bad little boy, haven't I, Your Highness?

QUEEN You certainly have, Grogan! Now, get up here with that behind! Come on, over my knee, you little bastard!

Grogan groans, gets over Queen's knee, and gets a spanking.

QUEEN Maybe this'll teach you to arouse royalty!

GROGAN *(Yelping)* Harder! Harder!

QUEEN *(Wildly in orgasm)* Ahhhhhhhhh!!

GROGAN *(Embarrassed)* May I get up, Your Majesty?

QUEEN *(Annoyed)* Yes, get up, stupid. I hope you didn't leave any pecker tracks on my gown.

GROGAN May I get dressed, Your Majesty?

QUEEN   Yes, please do. Your body has a certain odor about it that always annoys me.

GROGAN   An odor, Your Majesty?

QUEEN   Yes, a wretched stench!

GROGAN   I wash daily, Your Majesty.

QUEEN   Well, wash harder in the future. There is a noticeable odor zone *somewhere* on your body and I'd appreciate it if you could locate it and deodorize it!

FILMING A SPANKING

GROGAN   I will try and correct it, Your Majesty.

QUEEN   Oh, I know we all can't be perfect, Lieutenant Grogan. Come over here and sit by my feet.

GROGAN   I honor you, Queen Carlotta.

QUEEN   *You* honor me, but certain commoners in this town obviously don't! Someone threw a mudball at me today! Oh, if only I had a little pink button to push that could wipe out this town! Tell me—is it possible to get me a hydrogen bomb?

GROGAN   I doubt it, Your Majesty.

QUEEN   How about germ warfare, do you know anything about that?

GROGAN   You mean poisoning the population?

QUEEN   Yes. That sounds like a fun project. How about *rabies?* Could we spread that disease inexpensively?

GROGAN   I think so, Your Majesty. All we need is some rabid bat pus to make a serum.

QUEEN   Fine, let's try it. Rabid bat pus, and let's throw in some rat piss for good luck!

GROGAN   You are a genius, Your Majesty.

Enter Lieutenant Wilson and Goons carrying Princess Coo-Coo and Peggy in dog cages.

COO-COO *(Struggling, biting, shrieking)*   You let me out of here, Mummy! You murderess! You stinking Fascist slug!!

Soldier kicks cage.

GOON A *(To Peggy)* Bark for the Queen.

PEGGY Woof. Woof. Woof.

WILSON Your Majesty, Herbert the garbageman is dead
and . . . *(Indicating Peggy)* . . . thanks to this noble peasant woman, we have captured Coo-Coo and returned her
to the castle.

QUEEN Release the prisoners!

PEGGY *(Cowering, kneeling)* Thank you, Your Wonderful
Majesty.

COO-COO *(Being released)* You bilious ball of blubber . . .
you rotten, stinking . . . *(She runs and attacks Queen, soldiers pull her off)*

QUEEN THAT WAS THE LAST STRAW, COO-COO!
I hereby proclaim . . . *(Trumpets sound)* Oh, shut up! I
hereby proclaim that you are no longer the Princess of
Mortville! You will be gang-raped by my soldiers, injected
with rabies, and then exiled to the streets of Mortville,
where you belong!

COO-COO I consider that an honor, Your Royal Hogness,
to once and for all be freed from this mockery of a mon-
archy! I will never live down the shame of my inherited
name, but I will do my best to see that you topple from the
throne! *(Spits in her eye)*

QUEEN *(Enraged) (To soldiers)* Seize her and fuck her!

*Guards rush in, maul Princess, and drag her off screaming.
Peggy is trembling on floor.*

PEGGY   That was a courageous decision, Your Majesty.

QUEEN   You may stand, Mrs. Gravel. *(She does)* I appreciate your help in the capturing of my daughter. Loyalty to the Queen sometimes results in a reward.

PEGGY   Oh, let *me* be the new princess, Your Majesty! I have seen the human trash of Mortville and I share your contempt for this town!

QUEEN   My subjects are beneath contempt, Mrs. Gravel.

PEGGY   Dealing with poor people is a waste of time! Only the rich should be allowed to live!

QUEEN   I like your politics, Mrs. Gravel, and to be truthful, I need a woman like yourself to follow in my footsteps.

PEGGY   If you looked all over this land, I doubt you'd find a woman as vicious as I, Your Majesty.

QUEEN   We'll give you a trial run. Your first duty will be to help my soldiers spread rabies to everyone in this town. Do you think you can handle that?

PEGGY   Oh yes, Your Majesty!! And I know just the person I want to give it to first!!!

Cut to Mole leaving drugstore, counting lottery money.

She walks up street, snarling at people, and goes to Hopkins Hospital. She goes into Sexual Reassignment Clinic.

Mole enters waiting room. Sex changes and future sex changes are sitting around waiting.

RECEPTIONIST *(Entering)*   May I help you?

MOLE   Yeah, I want a sex change.

Everyone is shocked, embarrassed, coughing, etc.

RECEPTIONIST *(Rising)*   Could you step over here, please?

MOLE *(Goes over to desk)*   Hey, look, I'm in a rush so I'd appreciate it if you took me before these other turkeys.

RECEPTIONIST *(Whispering)*   Do you have an appointment?

MOLE   No, I don't!

RECEPTIONIST   I'm awfully sorry, we don't take anyone without an appointment.

MOLE *(Pulling knife on her)*   You do now, Nurse Nancy! Come on, bitch, cut these tits off!

RECEPTIONIST   I am only a nurse. The doctor isn't in now.

MOLE   Like hell he isn't!!

Grabs receptionist and pushes her into doctor's office. Doctor jumps up.

RECEPTIONIST   I'm sorry, Dr. Friedman.

MOLE   Come on, quack. I want the sex change and I want it fast!

DOCTOR *(Stammering)*   Why, madam, the sex change is a long, complicated process, we can't just . . .

MOLE   Just give me the basics, or I'll cut off her head!!

DOCTOR *(Pleading)*   Why don't you just fill out the necessary forms and we'll see if . . .

MOLE *(Jumps up on operating table)*   Cut the sermons and give me my wang! I want a wang and I want it NOW!

DOCTOR *(Approaching)*   I can only do so much under the circumstances. . . .

MOLE   IF YOU DON'T GIVE ME A SEX CHANGE, I'LL CUT OFF YOUR PETER AND SEW IT ON ME MYSELF!!!

DOCTOR *(Grabbing scalpel)*   I'll . . . see what I can do, madam.

≋≋≋

Cut to Mole's living room. Muffy is alone and nude, talking to her breasts.

MUFFY   Hi, big boys! I bet you didn't know that I won the Maryland lottery! Yes! I'm gonna be buying you lots of new push-up bras, so get ready for a new home! Yessiree, things are gonna be looking up for you two! . . .

Mole barges in with presents, dressed in a very masculine Superfly-type outfit.

MOLE   Well, howdy, Miss Muffy!

PARTY TIME

MUFFY *(Jumps up)* Oh Mole, you made it! *(They hug)* I was so worried about you! You got the money?

MOLE I sure do, Muffy. Look at these greenbacks!

MUFFY *(Eyes lighting up)* Oh Mole! Thank God, money at last! *(She starts kissing bills)* Beautiful germ-carrying American currency! What you got in all those shopping bags?

MOLE Presents, Muffy. Presents fit for a queen!

MUFFY Can I open 'em?

MOLE You sure can, you big hunk of beauty.

Muffy dives into presents. She opens lingerie box.

MUFFY   Oh, Mole, a new bra! It's just beautiful!

MOLE   Try it on. *(She does)* Here, let me help you!

MUFFY   Oh, that support feels heavenly! What else you got for me, Mole?

MOLE   Try this one, gorgeous. *(Hands her dress box)*

MUFFY *(Opening it)*   I feel like a little girl on Christmas morning! A gown!!!! *(Trying it on)* Oh, it's stunning! Thank God I was born a woman! I feel like a queen already, Mole!

MOLE   You will be queen, Muffy. I promise you. Look at these huggers. *(Takes out guns)*

MUFFY   Arms! Oh goody goody!

MOLE   This one's mine and this little .38's all for you, baby.

MUFFY *(Moved)*   You're so good to me, Mole, I don't know what I'd do without you.

MOLE   I got another surprise for you, Muffy. A real big surprise! Something you never even asked for!

MUFFY   A Chihuahua, Mole?

MOLE   No, you'll see—close your eyes! *(She does)* No peeking now! *(She takes down pants)*

MUFFY   Hurry, Mole! The suspense is killing me!

MOLE   You can open 'em now.

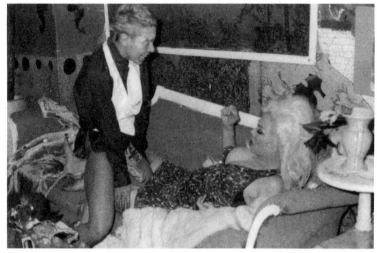

DYSFUNCTION

MUFFY *(Opens eyes and sees hideous phony sex-change penis)* Ahhhhhhhhh!!! *(Falling backwards, gagging)* What have you done to yourself?!?

MOLE *(Advancing)* I got the sex change just for you, Muffy. *(Tries to hump her)*

MUFFY *(Completely horrified)* Get off me with that ugly deformed worm! You're sick, Mole! You're a sick weirdo pervert!

MOLE Just let me try it once, Muffy, I gotta see if it works! It's a brand-new model, I got it at Hopkins Hospital!

MUFFY Cut it off, Mole. Rid your body of that disgusting transplant!

MOLE *(Pleading)* It never goes soft, Muffy!

MUFFY *(Vomits)*   Cut it off, Mole!!!

MOLE *(Grabbing a pair of scissors)*   So much for science, Muffy! *(Cuts it off)* Ahhhhhhhhhh!

Muffy screams, picks up sex-change penis off the dirty floor, and throws it out front door.

A mangy dog on the street immediately eats it.

Fade to Peggy in Coo-Coo's bedroom, dressed in black evil princess outfit, cutting up bats and rats and making a serum. Next to her is a rat in a cage. We hear it piss.

SPECIAL EFFECTS

RABIES FOR MORTVILLE

PINK FLAMINGOS AND OTHER FILTH

PEGGY   Well, finally! Some rat urine, just what the doctor ordered! *(Sucks it up in syringe and squirts it in serum)* That oughta give it a little kick! *(To Goon)* Bring in Princess Coo-Coo and tell her her *medicine's* ready!

Goons drag Coo-Coo in after gang rape. She struggles.

COO-COO   Don't touch me with those semen-stained hands, you big ape!!! I can walk by myself!!

PEGGY   Well, if it isn't Commoner Coo-Coo, the grave robber! All ready for your injection?

COO-COO   You ass-kissing little snitch! One day I'll get my hands on you.

PEGGY   I doubt you'll have the time. *(Gives her shot in ass)* Because you are now the proud owner of RABIES!!!

COO-COO GETS HER VACCINE

Shot of Coo-Coo being booted out of castle.

Coo-Coo tries to flee, goons raise drawbridge. She jumps to ground.

GOON 1   Hit the streets, scuz bag!

GOON 2   But don't bite anybody, dog face! Hahahahaha!

Cut to Muffy sewing up Mole's offscreen wound with dental floss. Mole is moaning in agony.

MUFFY   Be brave, sugar, be brave. I'll get you all fixed up.

MOLE   I thought you'd like it, Muffy. I thought you wanted a man!

MUFFY   I just said that to make you jealous, Mole. I liked your organs just fine the way they were.

MOLE   Now . . . now I won't have any organs. It'll be like having a Barbie Doll crotch.

MUFFY   Now, don't you worry—when I'm through with these stitches, it'll be close enough in my book.

MOLE   Will you . . . ever be able to love my operation?

MUFFY   I'll love it, Mole, I'll love it, feel it, and eat it, just like old times. Now hold on, this is gonna hurt. *(Rips stitches)*

MOLE   AHHHHHHHHHHHHHHHH!

A knock is heard at door.

MUFFY *(Aggravated)* Oh, who the hell is this? *(Impatiently answers the door)*

Flipper, Shotsie, Shina, and Coo-Coo come in. Coo-Coo is diseased and disheveled and has to be helped.

FLIPPER Hi, Your Majesty. *(Seeing Mole)* Holy shit, Mole, what happened to you?

MOLE *(Trying to act as if nothing is wrong)* Muffy just gave me an abortion.

SHOTSIE *You* were pregnant, Mole?

MOLE I wasn't going to tell anybody but . . . well, I was raped by the lottery officials when I picked up my money.

FLIPPER Men are such cunts!

SHINA Oh, men, women, they're all okay with me as long as they're NUDE!

SHOTSIE How many times we gotta tell you? Men are genetic rejects. All that gristle they got hanging between their legs was God's first big mistake and us women been paying for it ever since!

MOLE *(Glaring at the Princess)* What's SHE doing in my home?

FLIPPER Be easy on her, Mole. She's been through hell. When we found her, she was regurgitating in the streets.

SHOTSIE Her mother, the HOG, had her gang-raped!

SHINA   The poor thing's had a terrible time! *(To Mole)* You know that Gravel woman you were hanging out with? Well, she works for the Queen now; she shot Coo-Coo up with a rabies potion!

MOLE   I'm not surprised—that snotty little social climber! I knew I should have fractured her skull!

MUFFY *(To Coo-Coo, trying to be polite)*   Coo-Coo, can I get you anything? Are you infectious, sweetheart?

COO-COO   I don't know . . . I itch a lot and my saliva tastes funny.

MUFFY   Under the circumstances, I must ask you to refrain from using our kitchen utensils.

UNWELCOME HOUSE GUESTS—SHOTSIE, COO-COO,
SHINA (MARINA MELIN), FLIPPER

COO-COO   I won't breathe on anything—I promise. But please . . . help me kill my mother!

Cut to Queen and Peggy in Queen's bedroom. Queen is eating a stuffed pig. Peggy is getting a pedicure from Lieutenant Williams.

QUEEN *(To Peggy)*   How's Project Rabies coming along, Peggy?

PEGGY   Oh, I feel just like Jonas Salk. Tomorrow is our first day of mass immunization—or at least that's what the morons of Mortville think!

QUEEN *(Laughing)*   Oh, won't it be funny when they all start collapsing in the streets? It'll be like walking through a human sewer.

WILLIAMS   I hope I get a chance to kick every one of them right in the head just as they gasp for their last breath!

PEGGY   It'll be beautiful! A symphony of death rattles! *(Moved)* History will not forget this holiday of death!

Cut to Muffy and Mole, Shina, Shotsie, and Flipper sneaking up to castle with guns and knives. Mole walks in pain and Coo-Coo is dragged along in a state of advanced illness.

Shot of soldiers hanging around hallway, drunk and partying.

Shot of women hiding as Muffy exhibits herself to soldiers.

MUFFY   Hey, Officer Cutie-Pie. There's somebody down here to see you!

Shot of Goon seeing her, leering, and coming down to entrance.

GOON   What do you want, slut?

MUFFY *(Very suggestively)*   I'm looking for a little fun, officer. Can I come in and see your bedroom?

Goon is turned on and lowers drawbridge.

GOON *(Muttering to himself)*   I've had a hard-on for this bitch for a long time.

Shot of Mole et al. waiting to strike.

GOON *(Coming across bridge)*   You know you horny pigs aren't supposed to come cruisin' around the castle!

MUFFY   Oh, officer, it's just that you're so cute, I couldn't resist!

Goon starts mauling and kissing Muffy.

GOON   Yeah, you're a shapely little muvva.

Flipper and Shotsie run out and stab him in the back.

FLIPPER   One down, girls!

SHOTSIE   Good work, Muffy! Let's move quickly and quietly!

They sneak into castle with drawn guns.

*Shot of Goons dead drunk, looking at porno, making ob-
scene comments as Grogan dances for them drunkenly.
Mole rushes in with raised gun.*

MOLE   EAT LEAD, MOTHERFUCKERS!

*Flipper, Shina, Shotsie, and Muffy open fire on goons.
Cut to Queen's bedroom. Peggy hears gunshots.*

PEGGY   What's that, Your Majesty?

QUEEN   It's probably just the dumb soldiers playing Russian
roulette.

WILLIAMS *(Getting up)*   I'll go check it out, Your Majesty.

*As Williams begins to exit, gunfire is heard. He staggers
back into room, and collapses. Women come charging in.
Peggy screams. Flipper, Shotsie, Muffy, and Mole sur-
round Queen. Shina helps Coo-Coo.*

MOLE *(Aiming gun at Queen)*   Hold it right there, you royal
asshole.

QUEEN   Get out of my chamber, lesbians!

FLIPPER   You're through giving orders, meatball!

SHINA   You've humiliated us for the last time, warthog!

COO-COO *(Foaming, shaking)*   Let me bite her. Let me sink
my fangs into her fat little legs.

MOLE   Go right ahead, honey. Give her the chomp of life.

Coo-Coo advances, looking rabid. Queen panics.

The Goons Have a Ball . . .

. . . Briefly

QUEEN   Get away from me, child . . . you listen to your mother . . . I'm warning you!

Coo-Coo bites her leg.

QUEEN   AAAAHHHHHHHHHHHHH!

Coo-Coo slithers back, chuckling and foaming at mouth.

PEGGY *(A desperate attempt)*   Thank God, you've rescued me! I thought I'd never get out of here alive.

They all laugh in her face.

MOLE   Oh, come off it, pretty little Peggy. We all know what you been up to! I hope you're all ready for your little debutante party in hell—'cause that's where you're going!

PEGGY *(Panicked)*   You wouldn't kill a sister.

LIBERATION

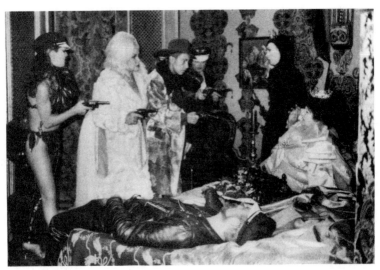

MOLE   Oh yes we would. How about it, girls? Should we give our "sister" a little rectal reminder that we don't like social climbers here in Mortville?

ALL   YEAH! GET HER!

Girls hold Peggy down and pull up her skirt. Mole puts gun to Peggy's ass.

MOLE   I'm gonna blow your bowels out!

PEGGY   Go ahead—a single gunshot cannot destroy the beauty of fascism! You're so low, you make white trash look positively top drawer!

MOLE   Ah, blow it out your ass!

Mole pulls trigger. Peggy flies across room.

QUEEN   You filthy muff divers will pay for this!

MOLE   Shut your fucking mouth!!

QUEEN   No dyke gives me orders!

MUFFY   Oh yeah, Queenie? Well, how does this grab you? Royal proclamation number one: KISS . . . MY . . . ASS!!

Queen balks.

MOLE   You heard the new queen—KISS IT!

Queen swallows hard.

ALL   KISS IT! KISS IT! KISS IT!

Queen kisses her ass.

MOLE *(Grabbing the Queen)* That's more like it, peon! Girls, how about it? I think the people of Mortville deserve a big feast to celebrate this great day of independence! We got ourselves the biggest turkey in the world—so why not EAT HER?!

ALL YEAH!

Dissolve to long shot of castle at night.

Mole appears atop castle.

MOLE Attention all Mortville residents! Queen Carlotta is dead! Your days of humiliation have come to an end!

Shot of Mortvillians exiting from their homes to listen.

MOLE To celebrate this joyous occasion I invite you to join me in a victory feast in honor of our newly found independence! Let the ring of freedom be heard all over this land —Mortville IS AT LAST A FREE CITY!!

Shot of Citizens cheering wildly, lighting torches. The drawbridge comes down and Muffy and Mole lead Shotsie, Flipper, Shina, and the dying Coo-Coo off the bridge carrying a huge platter. Queen Carlotta, cooked and garnished, is on the platter.

CITIZENS All hail the King! All hail the Queen!!

KISS MY ASS

Mole and Muffy blow kisses and bow royally.

Mole places Carlotta's crown on Muffy's head to thunderous applause.

Citizens begin eating the <u>Queen</u> with gusto.

Shot of Flipper, Shotsie, and Shina eating and laughing.

Shot of Coo-Coo trying to eat and foaming at the mouth. She finally drops dead.

Shot of Citizens hugging, laughing, and beginning to dance.

Muffy and Mole join in the celebration.

Muffy and Mole look extremely happy and kiss.

Long zoom-out shot of entire town dancing and celebrating.

Credit roll.

Flamingos Forever

Credit sequence.

Shot of skyline of Baltimore. Fifteen years later.

*Cut to close-up of highway sign—"Baltimore 10 miles."
Camera pans to Greyhound bus zooming by en route.*

*Tracking shot of front of Greyhound bus with destination:
"Baltimore."*

Interior bus—wide shot. Sailors, bums, assorted lowlife.

*Camera glides up aisle to lavatory door. It opens to reveal
Divine exiting. She looks astonishing in garish traveling
outfit, huge sunglasses, and scarf over hairdo. She sashays
down aisle, oblivious to glares from passengers, and stops
to sign autograph for tough black hoodlum. She takes her
seat and takes out huge compact, removing scarf to reveal
bizarre hairdo. She also takes off sunglasses to check elaborate eye makeup. Satisfied, she smiles to herself and looks
out window.*

*Camera pans over to Divine's sixty-five-year-old mother,
Edie, in next seat, dressed as a baby sucking a baby bottle.
She looks ridiculously happy and out of it until she spots a
soldier eating a hard-boiled egg, which throws her into a*

panicked trauma. Divine comforts her as camera glides one row forward to reveal Cotton II, a striking, but somewhat vacant, blond beauty. She intently watches a male passenger across the aisle who is reading Playboy. *She is voyeuristically turned on as she watchs his crotch, but he glances up, sees her, and shifts in embarrassment. Unfazed, Cotton II goes back to reading male nude magazine. Camera pans over to Crackers II, who is reading* Violent World Magazine *as Duane, an intense little boy with thick glasses, sits on his lap. Crackers II is a rough but very handsome hillbilly. Duane is about eight years old and is dressed in ridiculous bad drag. He is happily teasing the hair of a woman's wig he holds in his lap. Finishing the hairdo, he shows it to Crackers II, who helps Duane slip on the wig. Passengers glare in disgust. Duane models the wig happily and Crackers II hugs the happy child.*

Shot of sign—"Welcome to Baltimore, Your Charm City" —as Greyhound bus passes by.

Wide shot of Greyhound bus station. Usual poverty-stricken crowd is waiting for arriving bus. Sticking out like a sore thumb is the small pack of Divine groupies who are waiting with placards—"Welcome Home Filthiest," "15 Long Years," "We Are Filth," "Divine is God." They all wear tattooed F's on foreheads. They are: Bambi, a sexy Charo-type hillbilly; Inez, a beautiful tall fanatic; Irma, a bizarre high-fashion model; Doyle, a middle-aged, overly dressed Liberace type; and Wiffle and Waffle, two exhibitionist musclemen. The bus pulls in and groupies are wild with excitement. Bus door opens and passengers disembark and look confused at sight of groupies, who have pushed to the front of awaiting crowd. Finally Crackers II gets off, holding Duane. Groupies cheer, get his autograph, and touch him like some sort of god. Cotton II follows and Wiffle and Waffle start wildly tearing off their

*shirts and posing for her as she smiles in delight. Finally
Divine exits from bus, struggling with Mama Edie on her
back in baby backpack. Groupies go wild, falling to
ground. Inez rushes offscreen and comes back with giant
baby stroller and groupies struggle to put Edie in it. Filth
entourage is led out of bus station by Bambi, who throws
dead mackerels from a bucket to a stunned crowd of on-
lookers. Shot of filth family being led to extremely souped-
up Cadillac convertible with F-I-L-T-H vanity plates.
Crackers II is handed the keys and Edie is placed in a giant
baby seat with steering wheel in front seat. Cotton II rides
shotgun as Divine sits regally in backseat. Groupies pile in
another gaudy car and beckon them to follow. Cavalcade
pulls off.*

*Dissolve to cavalcade cruising down street in slum neigh-
borhood. Beggars, whores, and convicts rush from their
homes, falling to their knees as Divine blesses them and
throws kisses.*

*Dissolve to cavalcade riding through country. Car slows
up and Divine blows a kiss to a cow. The cow looks up
and runs.*

*Cavalcade drives on, turning down dirt road with signs
"Private Property—Keep Out," "No Assholes Allowed."*

End of credits.

*Shot of insane, multicolored, outlandish version of child's
tree fort with large deluxe store-bought swimming pool
below it.*

*Shot of Divine's face, awed at her new hideaway. All pile
out of cars, marveling at the beauty of their new home.*

BAMBI   From the filth followers all over the world—here it is! Your new hideaway!

DIVINE   It's absolutely PERFECT! I owe so much to you groupies; you who wear the F sign of filth on your foreheads for the whole world to see. Your work will not go unrewarded, I promise you!

Groupies oooohh and ahhh in excitement.

INEZ *(Proudly)*   Would you like to see the interior?

DIVINE   I'm waiting with bated breath, Inez.

DOYLE   This way, Madam Divine.

Groupies lead Divine and family to a rickety elevator at base of tree. The elevator rises to interior of tree fort.

Interior living room, a fantastic set, decorated in the most garish and hilarious way possible. They all enter.

DIVINE   Oooooohhh! It's beautiful.

COTTON II   So tasteful!

CRACKERS II   So luxurious!

IRMA   If I may point out, the living room offers complete video surveillance . . .

Shot of scanning video camera in corner of ceiling.

IRMA   . . . and playback system in case you and your family may want to review an especially stylish moment in your lives.

COTTON II   Are there any adult-oriented tapes available?

WIFFLE   This way, Miss Cotton II.

Wiffle and Waffle lead Cotton II into her bedroom, which is decorated with lurid male beefcake posters. A videotape machine and huge stack of male magazines and tapes is beside it. A single bed, lavishly made up, is the only furniture.

WAFFLE *(Pointing to porno)*   Every known male tape and magazine on the market, ma'am.

COTTON II *(Excited, turned on)*   Thank you . . . these are my boyfriends, you know. I meet them in pornographic magazines and videotapes and they live way deep in my brain . . . ready to take me out on dates whenever I need them. *(Looking through magazines)*

WIFFLE   Would you like a little show?

WAFFLE *(Flexing)*   That's what we're here for, you know.

COTTON II *(Wildly putting on tapes)*   No! Thank you anyway. I'll take a raincheck. . . . If . . . if I could be alone for a few minutes. . . .

Cut to Doyle and Divine pushing Edie in carriage into ridiculous, oversized nursery—huge Bathinette, bouncy chair, and one-sided baby crib, à la Baby Doll. *Divine and Doyle struggle to lift her into crib. She whimpers and begins sucking her thumb.*

DOYLE *(Looking at Edie, adoringly)*   Such a lovely woman. . . . Such a legend.

DIVINE   Ever since her divorce from the Eggman, her IQ has dropped to a low two figures. We hope that the move back to Baltimore will return her to her full intellectual capacity.

DOYLE   Great one, I am Mama Edie's top groupie in the world. I intend to fill her every moment with happiness.

DIVINE   Show her your love, Doyle, and show it unashamedly. She is a vast woman and her needs are monumental.

Cut to Crackers II being led by Bambi into his murder playroom. Guillotines, chainsaws, and drills are on torture rack. Life-sized blowup dolls are sitting in chairs in dungeonlike room.

CRACKERS II *(Calling out)*   Look at this, Mama!

Divine enters.

DIVINE   Your own little playroom, Crackers!

CRACKERS II   Oh God, Mama! A murder workshop! I can mutilate every single day! Morning—drill. *(Turns it on)* Afternoon—a chainsaw. *(Buzzes it)* . . . And evening—a blowtorch. *(Lights it)*

Duane enters in a panic.

DUANE   Mommy . . . Daddy . . . where are my pretty dresses?

BAMBI   If I may be so bold—the drag center is right off the master bedroom. This way, little Duane.

Bambi takes Duane's hand and leads him to tiny drag center. Divine and Crackers II follow and peer lovingly through doorway. Little makeup table, frilly decorations, racks of dresses, little-girl shoes, and in-scale ladies' hats. Duane is wild with joy, jumping on bed, trying on stupid hats, and struggling into frilly dresses. He peers into mirror, smears on lipstick, and turns to Divine, Crackers II, and Bambi.

DUANE *(Deadpan)* Snakes, snails, and puppy dogs' tails. That's what little boys are made of.

Crackers II and Divine rush to embrace him.

DIVINE We're going to be such a happy family here. . . . *(Turning coyly to Crackers II)* But Crackers II, my love . . . have you forgotten? We haven't seen our bedroom yet.

CRACKERS II *(Holding his crotch)* Oh, Mama, Mama!

BAMBI This way, Your Fabulousness.

Bambi, Divine, and Crackers II enter lavish master bedroom, with circular bed, mirrors, wild fabrics.

DIVINE *(Grabbing him)* Oh, my son, here is where we will fornicate in defiance of all natural laws. Here is where you will penetrate my motherhood so my M-spot quivers in ecstasy like a tuning fork.

Shot of Bambi, embarrassed to be present, looking disgusted.

CRACKERS II Oh, my mother, my wife, my eternal fleshpot.

They begin to embrace but Irma rushes in.

PINK FLAMINGOS AND OTHER FILTH

IRMA Excuse me, we've taken the liberty of kidnapping two journalists and bringing them here blindfolded. We thought a poolside press conference might be called for on this historic occasion of your return to Baltimore.

DIVINE *(Perking up. Primping excitedly)* The press? Already?

Cut to reporters being let out of trunk of the car by Wiffle and Waffle. Both reporters are handcuffed and wear black hoods.

AP Christ, what a way to get a story.

UPI UPI is never going to believe me.

AP Count your blessings. I covered Beirut and this is a *picnic* compared to that.

Reporters are led to poolside. Hoods and cuffs are removed. They rub their eyes and stretch.

INEZ *(From tree fort)* Gentlemen of the pencil press, get ready. I'm thrilled and proud to introduce the diva of your deadlines, the wow of the wire services, the high priestess of print, herself—The Filthiest Person Alive—DIVINE!

Shot of Divine descending on elevator in tiny leopard bikini. She poses wildly and reporters snap photos. Divine runs to poolside and does a huge cannonball. She surfaces exhibitionistically.

DIVINE Questions and answers!

UPI Phil Berkin, UPI. Why have you returned to Baltimore?

DIVINE *(Doing the breaststroke)* To live in harmony with my family and to work on my new book, tentatively entitled *Memoirs of a Goddess.* Get the title correctly, Mr. Berkin, and don't forget to SYNDICATE it!

Divine submerges in pool and we see her underwater, posing and swimming wildly. Divine shoots above water and begins doing militant butterfly stroke over to groupies by side of pool.

DIVINE *Why* is the European press not represented here? WHY, I ask?!

Groupies beg forgiveness. Doyle starts flogging himself.

AP Chris Como, Associated Press. Any men in your life?

DIVINE *(Treading water with hands raised)* There is only one man in my life—my husband, Crackers II, who you may remember is also my son.

UPI *(Appalled)* You're talking about incest?

DIVINE *(Doing backstroke)* I cannot begin to describe to you the genealogical miracle of producing a grandchild in my own little oven.

UPI Is the kid retarded?

DIVINE *(Doing sidestroke)* Another bourgeois myth handed down by generations of charlatans in the American Medical Association. My child is living proof of a new strain of heterosexuality.

AP On a lighter note, it looks like you've put on some weight.

DIVINE *(Snapping fingers as Bambi puts a piece of pie on small motorized serving tray and aims it toward Divine)* There is so much food, Mr. Como, and so little time.

Divine submerges with pie. Underwater we see her eat it. She comes up wiping her mouth.

DIVINE Give me more questions and I'll give you more answers!

UPI Didn't you eat dog shit once for publicity?

DIVINE *(Climbing out of pool)* Ah, UPI remembers my humble beginnings. A girl has to start somewhere, Mr. Berkin. I was a mere pebble of filth in the old days. But that pebble grew into a rock. And that rock kept on rolling through the sewers of society until it became a boulder. I guarantee you that boulder has become an AVALANCHE.

She shakes her body dry as reporters are soaked.

AP Where have you been for fifteen years?

DIVINE *(Now posing on diving board)* We lived in gas-station lavatories in Boise, Idaho, until my fans discovered me and refused to let me live unnoticed. With the help of those troops I opened a string of day-care centers for the children of armed robbers. But in my maturity, my autumn years, if you will, I have decided to give up this charity work and live like all world leaders, financially secure, surrounded by zombie worship and bathed in the constant glare of publicity.

Groupies have wheeled over fireworks display and light fuses. Divine models wildly for press on diving board as fireworks light up "WELCOME HOME DIVINE." Slow fade-out.

Slow fade-in to Venninger house—Victorian minimansion with sign: "Venninger Funeral Home." Camera slowly zooms to upstairs window.

Dissolve to Vera Venninger seated in front of dressing table, staring as if in a trance. She is evilly and severely made up, overdressed, and appears every inch the villainess.

VERA   Mirror, mirror on the wall, who's the filthiest of them all? *(No response)* Mirror, mirror on the wall! Who's the filthiest of them all? *(No response)* DAMN IT! COME IN! MIRROR, MIRROR ON THE WALL! WHO'S THE FILTHIEST OF THEM ALL?

Connie Marble's face fades in to mirror surrounded in flames. She has bright red hair and wears harlequin glasses.

CONNIE   You are, Vera! You are the filthiest person alive!

VERA   Oh, Connie, I will avenge your death!

CONNIE   Vera, my sister, only you, my flesh and blood, can claim the title of filthiest! STOP DIVINE BEFORE IT'S TOO LATE! I'M BURNING IN HELL BECAUSE OF HER!

Flames consume her and image fades out.

VERA   Connie, come back! Come back, my filthiest! *(No response) (She gets up in huff and gets large-sized home-*

made Divine devil doll) I'll get you, Divine, and your retarded little family too! *(Sticking pins into it)* Welcome
home, Divine! Welcome home, YOU FAT PIG!

*Cut to shot of Vera's husband, Wilbur Venninger, ghou-
lishly handsome, formally attired funeral director, in his
basement parlor, talking to two clients.*

WILBUR *(Pointing to casket)*   Believe me, this is the cheapest
casket you're going to find.

MRS. ASHBURN *(Without blinking)*   We'll take it.

MR. ASHBURN   We're trying to keep the expense to a bare
minimum.

WILBUR   Naturally—that's our specialty here at Venninger's. Cheapo funerals for the relatives that got on your
nerves.

MRS. ASHBURN   Oh, she was a bitch all right.

WILBUR *(Grabbing clipboard)*   Let's get the red tape out of
the way. *(To Mrs. Ashburn)* What did you say your mother's name was?

MR. ASHBURN   Hilda Helinski. Royal pain in the ass.

We hear Vera's voice booming through intercom system.

VERA   Wilbur! Wilbur!

WILBUR   If you'll excuse me for a second. *(He approaches
intercom system and flicks on switch)* Yes, my love?

Shot of Vera upstairs speaking into intercom.

VERA My groupie is supposed to be here any second. And we have *business* to take care of in case you forgot!

Cut back to Wilbur.

WILBUR I'm with some customers.

VERA That's all you ever think about! Your dead little things! You morgue rat!

Shot of Ashburns looking puzzled.

WILBUR Be right up, dear. *(Clicking off) (To Ashburns)* Sorry for the interruption. That's my wife. Sometimes she gets lonely at the top.

MR. ASHBURN *(Confused)* Who's your wife?

WILBUR Miss Vera Venninger.

MRS. ASHBURN I never heard of her.

MR. ASHBURN Me either.

WILBUR *(Proudly)* She's the filthiest person alive!

Ashburns look confused and shrug.

MR. ASHBURN See you at the service, Mr. Venninger. *(Starts to exit)*

WILBUR Wilbur to you, folks.

MRS. ASHBURN Just remember, Wilbur, *no frills!* *(They exit)*

Wilbur rubs his hands together excitedly and approaches trash can and takes off lid to reveal Hilda Helinski's corpse. He slams lid back on and starts playing peek-a-boo with head, laughing insanely.

Cut to shot of Vera Venninger unlocking huge padlock on attic dungeon door.

Shot of Tracy and Jimmy, two zombied-out seven-year-olds clutching each other on filthy mattresses in kiddie dungeon. Both wear cute school outfits, now tattered and torn.

VERA *(Struggling with lock)* Hot buttered beans come to supper! *(She enters)* Good afternoon, my filthy little children.

TRACY & JIMMY *(Slavishly)* Good afternoon, Mrs. Venninger.

TRACY Mrs. Venninger, I feel sick.

JIMMY It's that stuff in the needles you give us.

VERA I *told* you all filthy little children take heroin and love it! Doesn't anybody appreciate anything I do for them? I give you all the candy you could possibly eat.

JIMMY My teeth hurt.

TRACY I want to go to the dentist.

VERA You never have to take baths and are forbidden to wash behind your ears!

TRACY But I itch!

JIMMY   I stink!

TRACY   I want to go to Bible school.

VERA   Complain. Complain. Complain. I've been in this room for at least thirty seconds and has either one of you lit up a cigarette?

Tracy and Jimmy obediently take out cigarettes and light them, coughing.

TRACY   But we're going to get cancer!

VERA   Inhale, Tracy. Take it deep into your lungs. Go ahead, Jimmy, hot-box it!

Both inhale deeply and cough.

VERA   That's better! Today is your first big test, you know. A young groupie is coming over today who happens to think I am the cat's meow. I plan on showing you off. If I were you, I'd be on my worst behavior!

JIMMY   We'll say what you tell us, Mrs. Venninger. But then, can we go home?

TRACY   We won't tell anybody you stole us!

VERA   I told you to stop nagging me about home! Any more of this crybaby sniveling and I'll make you go cold turkey!

JIMMY *(Shivering)*   What's cold turkey?

TRACY *(Optimistic)*   Are we gonna get pets? *(Crying)* I want my mommy!

VERA *(Taking out hypo needle and holding it up)*   Here's your mommy, little Tracy.

TRACY   Oh, please, not the needle again!

VERA *(Approaching her) (Mimicking her voice)* Not the needle again. I want my mommy. I want my mommy.

JIMMY *(Eyes lighting up, licking lips)*   Me first, Mrs. Venninger. Please give it to me first.

Cut back to Wilbur, who has removed Mrs. Helinski's corpse to an upright seated position. He has his arm around her, reading aloud a book of love sonnets as he cuddles her and pecks her cheek with kisses. Doorbell is heard. Wilbur pats her head and exits to answer.

Outside, a nervous Bambi is ringing the bell and looking over shoulder. Wilbur answers.

WILBUR   Come in, Bambi.

Interior Venninger living room.

BAMBI   I hope I'm not late. I came as soon as I could get away. They think I'm out delivering press releases.

WILBUR   Good work, Bambi. Can I get you something to eat? Are you by any chance a braunschweiger enthusiast? We have some. Fresh from the market!

BAMBI   No thank you, I had some delicious scrapple earlier.

WILBUR   Have a seat. *(Calling upstairs)* Oh, Vera, your number one groupie is here!

VERA *(Calling down)*   Tell her I'm about ready to make my grand entrance.

WILBUR *(To Bambi)*   Ladies and gentlemen! Miss Vera Venninger.

Vera comes down steps in affected entrance. Bambi applauds enthusiastically and rushes over, bends down, and kisses her feet.

BAMBI   Mrs. Venninger, I wear the F sign of filth only for you. *(On knees)* Others have allowed themselves to be brainwashed by Divine's egomaniacal behavior but I recognize the true leader of the filth movement to be you and only you.

VERA   Fear not, my disciple. Off your knees! *(Bambi rises)* My husband and I take the responsibility of filth seriously. With the help of your excellent espionage work, Divine will be humiliated and finally EXTERMINATED!

BAMBI   Amen! Amen!

VERA   Now, you must meet the little lost children. I'm quite proud of my youthful rehabilitation program. *(Flicks on loudspeaker)* Okay, brats! Get down here, double time!

Tracy and Jimmy enter looking doped up but still shy.

VERA   This is Bambi, my children. Go ahead, you know what to do.

JIMMY *(As in a child's recital. Takes bow)*   I hate my stupid parents and one day I'm going to burn down their house. I want to be a mass murderer when I grow up. . . . I . . . *(He forgets his lines and looks at Vera for prompting. She points to her eyeballs)* Oh, yes, I want to shoot heroin in my eyeballs! *(He bows and everyone politely applauds)*

VERA   That was lovely, Jimmy. Tracy, all ready?

TRACY   I can't wait to be a teen-ager so I can get my driver's license and become a drunk driver! I want to get every social disease so I can spread it to minority groups as soon as they get laid off their jobs. More than anything, I hope nuclear war breaks out!

Everyone applauds.

VERA   Charming, Tracy, just charming. Now I want you both to run along upstairs and play with your needles.

They rush out.

VERA *(To Bambi)*   Isn't child rearing satisfying?

BAMBI   I'm awed at the good work you're doing here, Mrs. Venninger.

VERA *(Suddenly rising)*   I'm afraid I cannot donate another second of my busy filth schedule, Bambi. I want you to immediately return to Divine's and let us know the instant she leaves her house. We have a little surprise for her, don't we, Wilbur?

WILBUR *(Eyes lighting up)*   Phase one, Vera?

VERA   The Final Divine Solution!

Wipe shot to Wilbur and Vera driving in big black limousine. Vera sits in the back as Wilbur drives.

VERA   Turn left here. *(Checking watch)* Three-thirty. School will just be letting out. All we need is one more child, Wilbur, and the Children's Crusade will be ready for AC-TION!

Shot of school kids happily leaving school. Limousine pulls up to corner where kids are jumping rope.

Shot of Vera evilly peering out window. One kid says good-bye to chums and starts skipping up the street. Evil soundtrack as Venninger car creeps up street tracking Kid. Vera's window comes down.

VERA   Hi!

Kid glances up, looks nervous and walks quicker.

VERA   What's your name?

KID *(Not looking at her)*   Larry.

VERA   Larry, how do you like this car?

KID *(Still walking, glances at it nervously)*   It's neat.

VERA   I have a secret to tell you.

KID   I'm not supposed to talk to strangers.

VERA   You don't want to know my secret?

KID *(Stops. Curious)*   What is it?

VERA *(Whispers)*   I know where E.T. is.

KID *(Excited)*   He's here?!

VERA   Yes. . . . Would you like to meet him? He's feeling awfully lonely.

KID *(Excited)*   You really know where E.T. is?!

VERA   Yes, come on, get in. He sent me out to look for friends.

KID *(Looking around, unsure)*   Will you get me home in time for dinner?

VERA   Of course. . . . Your parents will never even know.

Kid jumps in car.

Suddenly all the door locks go down automatically.

VERA *(Changing diabolically)*   WE'LL SEE WHO'S THE FILTHIEST PERSON ALIVE, LITTLE LARRY, WE'LL JUST SEE!!

Shot of horrified Kid trying to get out as Vera grabs him and handcuffs him to door handle.

Exterior shot as limo peels out.

Evening.

Cut to shot of Divine sitting in master bedroom with Duane in her lap. Divine is putting on final touch of his eye makeup. Divine wears large Kleenex boxes for shoes.

DIVINE   There. All finished. Now, Grandmommy has to get to work on her book, honey.

DUANE *(Pleading)* I'll be good. Just let me stay in your lap.

Divine pets him and reaches for tape recorder. She flicks it on.

DIVINE Testing 1-2-3-4. *(Plays it back)* "Testing 1-2-3-4." *Memoirs of a Goddess.* Chapter One. "Roots of Filth." Like most goddesses, I was born in humble surroundings. Little did my parents know that their newborn, weighing in at a rather impressive eighteen pounds, would grow up to be internationally celebrated for her beauty, style, and fashion flair. *(Plays it back)* ". . . beauty, style, and fashion flair."* (Tapes again)* Correction. Beauty, style, *motherhood*, and fashion flair.

Duane smiles and cuddles up to her.

Cut to Crackers II in his murder playroom, hiding behind chair with knife as he watches two blowup dummies sitting in front of cardboard box with TV screen crudely drawn on it.

CRACKERS II The crazed psychopath has escaped from the mental institution and he has but one thing on his mind— SPLATTER! *(He sneaks up on dummies)* The people are so preoccupied with television they don't even hear him enter the house. *(Crackers II puts Alka-Seltzer in mouth and slurps it around, making foam)* Foaming at the mouth, he springs into action! Okay, you two, stay right where you are! *(Imitating couple and jumping back and forth in different roles)* "Please don't hurt my TV set!" "Have mercy on our souls!" The maniac has flashbacks to all the television violence he saw as a child. Unable to control his urge to kill, he ignores the victims' pleas and begins a whirlwind of carnage! AHA! *(He stabs dummies, pours ketchup into weird machine he has built that pumps fake blood)* Oh, God! No, no, no! *(Switching roles)* How about the chainsaw? *(Turns it on and begins cutting up dummies)* NOOoooo! *(Puts steak and liver into meat grinder and turns handle as other ridiculous machine pours guts out)* *(Crackers II goes wild, jumping back and forth laughing hysterically)*

Cut to shot of Cotton II, sitting on bed in beautiful loungewear. She is voyeuristically ecstatic as Wiffle and Waffle slowly do striptease.

WIFFLE   Next comes the shirt, Miss Cotton II.

COTTON II *(Panting)*   Yes . . . yes. Slowly, Wiffle. Waffle! Flex those pecs.

Wiffle and Waffle pose in all sorts of ludicrous ways.

WAFFLE   I work out just for you. You're the only person that sees my muscles.

COTTON II *(Thrashing on bed, hiding her face with pillow, then looking up wilder)*   Yes . . . I know, I know. Be careful not to brush up against me. *(Frustrated, she picks up porno magazine and starts frantically turning the pages, then throws it down)* Damn this porno! It's all used up! There's nothing more frustrating than USED porno!

WIFFLE   How about this, Miss Cotton II!

They begin wrestling.

COTTON II   Yes! Go! Go! Go! Let me see the inside of your thighs! *(Impatiently)* Take those goddamn pants off! *(They do. One wears jock, the other Jockey shorts)* Oh, God, I'm getting ready! Get me my voyeur booth!

FLAMINGOS FOREVER

Wiffle and Waffle rush to closet and bring out specially made voyeur booth. It is large cardboard box, festively decorated, that slips over Cotton II's entire body, except feet. It features a windshield and wipers. She struggles and is helped into it, moaning in pleasure.

Wiffle and Waffle do finals of exhibitionist poses as Cotton II staggers around room in climax. Booth steams up and windshield wipers go on.

Cotton II collapses in faint.

Voyeur booth topples over.

Cut to Edie on Bathinette in nursery as Doyle pins on her diaper and slips on rubber pants over top.

Edie is gurgling happily.

DOYLE   There we go. All cleaned up. Would little Edie like to get in the bouncy chair? *(Edie nods and gurgles excitedly)* I thought you would! *(She gets in oversized bouncy chair and starts bouncing)* Fun, isn't it? Yes, poor little Edie's had a rough time, hasn't she? But she's gonna be all better soon. *(Edie gurgles)* Would you like me to read to you? *(Edie bounces faster and nods)* *(Doyle returns with big book)* How about this? *The Story of Communism.* "In 1848 Karl Marx published 'The Communist Manifesto.'" *(Edie looks excited, eager)* "There were three fundamental ideas in this work." *(Edie holds up three fingers)* That's right, Edie! Three! You're doing great, old girl! "Number one: Class struggle can only be ended by the victory of the working class." *(Edie soberly makes struggling motions and then raises arms in victory)* That's fabulous, Edie. You understood! "Number two: The working class will and must become the ruling class." *(Edie wildly applauds and almost bounces out of her chair)* Amazing! "... And, finally, there can be no half measures. WORKERS OF THE WORLD, UNITE!" *(Edie goes wild, bouncing, applauding, weeping in victory) (Doyle hugs her)* You're gonna be all right, Edie. Forget those eggs, you're gonna be a Communist!

Cut to Divine continuing her memoirs. Duane is fast asleep in her lap.

DIVINE *(Into microphone)* To the outside world, my parents were normal people. But their unwholesome obsession with cleanliness made my life as a little girl unmitigated hell. For all appearances, my mother was a normal housewife, but her house could never be clean enough.

Flashback shot. Divine's memoirs continue as voiceover. We see Chesty, Divine's mother, dressed in bra and toreador pants as she scrubs the kitchen floor. She has the largest breasts on earth.

DIVINE ... My father was a butcher by trade and he, too, was consumed by a phobia against dirt.

Shot of Tubby, Divine's father, the ultimate low-rent Vegas type. He is furiously vacuuming the furniture.

DIVINE ... I longed for a normal childhood, but my parents could not let me be.

Shot of Baby Divine, a plump little girl trying to read the book The Three Pigs *as she sits uncomfortably dressed in overstarched party dress.*

Chesty and Tubby eye her with fury as they continue to clean.

DIVINE   . . . My skin was raw from the starch my mother insisted on putting in my dresses. I had to wash my hair every hour on the hour.

Shot of Chesty violently washing Baby Divine's hair in bubble bath as Baby Divine screams.

DIVINE   . . . And brush my teeth fifty times a day.

Shot of Tubby holding Baby Divine by force as he painfully brushes her teeth.

DIVINE *(Miserably)*   . . . My parents were The Cleanest People Alive . . .

Shot of Baby Divine reading contently as Tubby and Chesty sneak up on her with vacuum cleaner and scrub bucket.

DIVINE   . . . and their cleanliness abuse was cruel and never-ending.

Shot of Tubby attacking Baby Divine by vacuuming her. Chesty grabs her also and begins scrubbing her with Mr. Clean and scrub brush. Baby Divine screams in horror.

DIVINE   . . . Finally my parents decided I was too filthy to live in their house. They concealed me in a trash can and dropped me on the doorstep of a total stranger and I became . . . an orphan.

Shot of Chesty and Tubby lugging garbage can down slum street. They leave it on step.

DIVINE ... They didn't even bid their only child farewell, but instead left me with one final indignity—a sign that read "Wash Me."

Tubby pins the sign to trash can and rings bell. They both run away.

DIVINE ... As fate would have it, a wonderful woman opened that door. A woman that would adopt me and become the real mother I never had.

Shot of Edie, with teeth, looking glamorous, coming to door, seeing trash can, opening it, and embracing Baby Divine.

Cut back to Divine in bedroom breaking down, sobbing at this memory. Suddenly a red sign saying "F-O-O-D" starts blinking on and off on bedroom wall. She jumps up excitedly, pulling herself together.

DIVINE Oh ... calories! *(Exits hurriedly)*

Wide shot of dinner table with Cotton II and Crackers II at table and Edie being placed in highchair. Wiffle, Waffle, and Irma gather around excitedly to watch them eat. Divine clomps in still wearing Kleenex boxes on feet, with Duane, and takes her place at head of the table.

DIVINE Doesn't it feel fabulous to be home again?

CRACKERS II Oh, Mama, Baltimore *is* best.

COTTON II All I can say is that I'm feeling much more relaxed. Wiffle and Waffle gave me quite a workout this morning. My eyeballs are simply scorched.

Inez serves turkey.

DIVINE That's wonderful, Cotton II. Pass the Hershey sauce, Crackers II. *(He does. She pours it all over turkey)*

ALL Mmmmmmmm.

DIVINE *(Winking at Duane)* Duane's been such a good little drag queen today, haven't you, honey?

DUANE Yes, Mommy, but I need some new frocks. I'm sick of yesterday's fashions. If I'm real good do you think I could get a bra?

CRACKERS II He deserves it, Mama. He's been so nelly lately.

DIVINE All in good time, my son.

Inez puts down huge bowl of mashed potatoes. Divine sprinkles chocolate jimmies over them. Everyone is eating.

COTTON II Inez, isn't there any salad? I want it *with* the meal, not after. We're hardly in France.

INEZ *(Putting down salad)* Yes, ma'am.

Cotton II sprays whipped cream on it and passes it around.

Doyle is feeding Edie in highchair.

DOYLE Madam Divine, Edie has been extremely mentally alert today. I've been reading to her about communism.

DIVINE That's exciting, Doyle. You happy, Mama?

EDIE   Workers of the World, Unite!

All are astonished and break into applause.

COTTON II   Did you hear that? She's talking!

DUANE   She's growing up!

CRACKERS II   She's politically aware!

COTTON II   She's a Communist!

DIVINE   Mama, being home really helps, doesn't it? You're gonna be all right.

DOYLE   I'll devote my every second to this wonderful senior.

DIVINE   Doyle, you will be rewarded for this, I promise you. Matter of fact—Inez, Irma, Wiffle, Waffle—I think you've had enough privileged glimpses of us eating. If you wish to continue your viewing, I must ask you to leave the room and watch through the peephole. Doyle, you stay right where you are.

DOYLE   Thank you, Divine.

Groupies exit scowling at Doyle jealously. Wiffle and Waffle try posing for Cotton II.

COTTON II   Later Wiffle, later Waffle. Can't you see I'm eating? Don't be disgusting.

Goupies go behind wall and watch through peephole.

CRACKERS II   Hey, Edie, I got an idea. You feel like doing the Hokey Pokey?

COTTON II   Yeah! The Hokey Pokey!

DIVINE   You taught it to me, Mama, when I was a little girl.

EDIE *(Excited)*   Hokey Pokey! Hokey Pokey! Hokey Pokey!

They all get up and form circle.

DIVINE   Ready? You put your right arm in, you put your right arm out. . . . *(All join in)* You do the Hokey Pokey and you turn yourself around. That's what it's all about!

DUANE   Left arm!

ALL   You put your left arm in . . . *(etc.)*

Shot of groupies peering through holes, marveling.

DIVINE   Come on, Mama!

EDIE   Left leg!

ALL *(Building in intensity)*   You put your left leg in . . . *(etc.)*
THAT'S WHAT IT'S ALL ABOUT!!!

Slow fade-out.

Slow fade-in to Venninger house.

Morning. We see paper boy coming down street throwing papers on porches. Wilbur opens the door at the exact time his paper is thrown and it hits him on head. He curses paper boy, who laughs at him. Wilbur picks up paper,

PINK FLAMINGOS AND OTHER FILTH

opens it, and sobs as he sees headline: "Divine Is Back! Filthier Than Ever!" He rushes to intercom.

WILBUR   Vera! Vera! *(Sobbing)* You should see the morning paper!

Cut to Vera in bedroom as she smashes radio against the wall.

She rushes to intercom.

VERA *(Furiously)*   It's on the radio too! It's starting again! She's stealing publicity that is rightfully ours! Oh, God, Wilbur, suppose she made the New York papers?

WILBUR   Nonsense, Vera. It's only local news.

VERA   We don't know that, do we, Wilbur? Go to the news-stand and get the New York papers!

WILBUR   You're the filthiest, Vera!

VERA   Not according to the press I'm not. Please get those papers! I think I'm having one of my publicity break-downs.

Wipe shot to Wilbur pulling up front at newsstand. He double parks, holding up traffic, and runs into store.

Interior newsstand. Close-up of New York Post—*"Filth Goddess Kidnaps the Press."*

Wilbur screams in shock.

Other customers turn to look at him. Frantically he searches around shop until he finds the Daily News *with headline "Divine to World, 'I'm Filthiest.'"*

Wilbur clutches his heart and falls to knees sobbing.

Gruff News Dealer approaches him.

NEWS DEALER   You all right, buddy?

WILBUR *(Sobbing)*   Do you carry *The New York Times?*

NEWS DEALER   What's your problem? You want me to call an ambulance?

WILBUR   No . . . no. . . . Please, I'd like a copy of *The New York Times.*

News Dealer shakes his head in disgust and hands him the Times. Wilbur frantically searches through first section, stops, and lets out a howl.

WILBUR   God, no! No! No! Not *The New York Times.* *(Falling to knees and weeping)* Not the fucking *New York Times.*

NEWS DEALER   You gonna buy these papers? This ain't a library, you know!

Cut to Vera Venninger in her bedroom, frantically setting up camera to take her own picture. She runs across room and grabs a bowl with tin foil on it.

VERA   Now, the filthiest person alive will eat dog shit for the world to see! *(Unwraps bowl)* This photo will prove that Vera Venninger is every bit as filthy as Divine! *(Takes out turd, nervously, squeamishly)* Ten seconds. Mmmmmm, dog shit! Eight seconds. My favorite snack. I eat it every day. Four seconds. Here she goes. *(Gets it close to face, gags, and turns head away)* Two seconds. *(Tries to eat it but is unable. She retches and camera flash goes off. She throws turd against wall and collapses in sobs)* I can't do it! I just can't do it!

Wilbur rushes in looking grim and defeated, carrying papers.

WILBUR   Vera, I'm afraid I've got bad news.

VERA   She got out-of-state coverage, didn't she?

WILBUR   All three New York papers.

VERA *(Horrified)*   *The New York Times?*

WILBUR   "People in the News" column.

VERA   Nooooo!

WILBUR   We did get *some* coverage. The *Baltimore Sun* has a small article about our child snatching.

VERA   What page, though? What page!!?

WILBUR   Well . . . page twenty-eight, but he's only been missing one day.

VERA   I'm sick of page twenty-eight! My whole life has been page twenty-eight! *(Desperately)* Oh, Wilbur, make love to me.

WILBUR   I . . . I . . . Oh, Vera, you know I'm a sexual dysfunctionist.

VERA   Just because I'm not a corpse! It's not fair! Please! I'll be dead for you tonight, my darling. *(She runs and gets ice bucket)* I'll put ice on my skin! *(Starts rubbing it on her arms)* Feel. Go ahead. My flesh will be colder than death!

WILBUR *(Excited, unsure)*   Will you get in a body bag?

VERA *(Quickly)*   Yes! Yes!

Wilbur rushes from room. Vera goes into fake rigor mortis as Wilbur rushes back in with body bag. Vera gets in and Wilbur begins to be aroused. Vera is holding her breath with all her might. Wilbur starts kissing her. He takes off shirt and gets in bag. We see Vera begin to panic as she stifles a sneeze. Suddenly, she can hold it no longer and loudly sneezes. Wilbur jumps up appalled.

VERA   I'm sorry!

WILBUR   You ruined it!

VERA   Start over! I swear I won't sneeze again.

WILBUR *(Panicked)*   It's no good, Vera. I know you're not a corpse! A corpse never wants reciprocation! Never, Vera! I have to finish off downstairs. *(He rushes out)*

VERA   No, Wilbur! *(She throws self on bed, sobbing)*

Shot of Wilbur in funeral room, disrobing in a hurry. He opens coffin containing same rotting corpse and jumps in and slams lid shut. Casket rocks back and forth, intercut with Vera under the covers sobbing and rubbing herself in sexual frustration. Wilbur cries out in orgasm. Vera is about to climax but phone rings.

VERA   God damn it! *(Answers)* HELLO!

Shot of Bambi in phone booth.

BAMBI   Mrs. Venninger, did I catch you at a bad time?

VERA   What *is* it, Bambi?

BAMBI   The time has come for action! The tree fort is empty! The entire Divine family is headed downtown.

VERA *(Suddenly power-crazed)*   Oh, finally I can start my aggression! *(Beginning to fondle herself again under the covers as she goes into fantasy tirade)* After Divine is humiliated and destroyed, Maryland will be ours! We attack Delaware and blow up the Delaware Memorial Bridge.

Superimposed war maps of East Coast. Animated tanks and planes advance, blowing up cities as she talks.

VERA *(Excited, panting)*   Our troops will plunder north, conquering Philadelphia until we reach the New Jersey border. . . .

Superimposed cliché stock footage of war, bombs, planes.

Shot of Bambi listening in phone booth, looking confused and embarrassed.

VERA *(Wildly turned on)*   . . . In two swift surprise air raids Trenton and Newark will fall and then—like the last domino—New York City will lie before us. Ready to be leveled by our highly skilled kamikaze pilots! . . .

Superimposed shot of nuclear bomb explosion.

VERA *(Moaning, climaxing)*   . . . And FINALLY I will take my rightful place in filth history—the undisputed, highly feared DICTATOR OF FILTH, THE GREAT ONE, VERA VENNINGER!

Cut to shot of happy Divine family in one car and groupies in another as they pile out in downtown Baltimore.

Divine starts posing to dumbfounded passersby and crowd gathers to gawk. Groupies start working the crowd.

INEZ *(To Bum)*   Hello, sir. Isn't she something?

BUM   She's a fat one, all right.

INEZ *(Pulling out large locket with photo of Divine)*   Would you be interested in purchasing a magic locket blessed with a picture of Divine? It has the power to ward off all evil curses and hoodoo. . . .

Divine is modeling wildly as Edie, Crackers II, and Cotton II sign autographs. Wiffle and Waffle circulate through crowd with collection boxes on long handles.

Crowd puts in money.

Cut to Irma trying to sell an older Lady a locket.

IRMA   It's only $9.95—a real bargain in these inflationary times.

LADY   Get away from me! I know all about you Moonies. You're brainwashed and you should be deprogrammed!

IRMA   Madam, I'm certainly *not* a Moonie. . . . I'm a Divinity!

Cut to Divine ending her little show and kissing her family good-bye as they all go their separate ways.

Edie is helped into giant stroller.

Divine begins walking down the street.

Shot of motorist gawking at her from behind wheel. Divine notices and puts on a show for him. He is so intent on staring that he doesn't look where he's going and smashes into telephone pole. Divine blows kisses at him as he angrily leaps from car.

Cut to shot of Cotton II, extremely happy, window-shopping in front of dirty book shop on The Block, Baltimore's porno district.

She enters and approaches grubby clerk.

COTTON II   Excuse me.

CLERK   Yeah?

COTTON II   Where's your all-male section?

CLERK *(Looking at her skeptically)*   Next to bondage, on the left.

COTTON II   Well, actually, maybe you could help me. There's two particular titles I'm interested in. Do you have *All About Balls?*

CLERK   Jesus Christ almighty.

COTTON II   The other one I read a great review of recently —*100 Asses: Eat 'Em, Pump 'Em.*

CLERK   Lady, look, we got what you see. That's about it.

COTTON II   Would it be possible to special-order them?

CLERK   You Vice or something?

COTTON II *(Insulted)*   Why, no! I'm a Woman for Pornography!

Cut to shot of preteen girls' clothing shop. Duane is trying on a bra as horrified saleslady looks on. Crackers II helps him slip on panty girdle. Duane is thrilled and tries to leave dressing room to look in mirror. Saleslady is panicked, tries to block his way, but Duane gets past her as other girl shoppers see him and scream. They run from store with mothers.

Cut to shot of Doyle pushing Edie into Left Wing Bookshop. Edie is waving to serious radical customers, who glare back in disgust. Edie points to book The Story of Karl Marx *and goes wild.*

Dissolve to Doyle reading to Edie in children's playground. Edie slides down sliding board and gets on swings. Curious children point and laugh.

DOYLE   "Free man and slave, patrician and plebian, lord and serf—in a word, oppressor and oppressed—"

EDIE *(Interrupting)*   Oh, Doyle, I know that part. What I wanna know is—WAS KARL MARX CUTE?

DOYLE   Here's a picture, Miss Edie, decide for yourself.

Edie looks at photo.

EDIE *(Giggling)* Oh, he's adorable! That Karl Marx is a regular little doll baby! *(Troubled)* But, Doyle, was Karl Marx filthy?

DOYLE That's a major historical question, Edie. Only time can tell that.

EDIE Could Karl Marx be my new boyfriend?

DOYLE Why, Edie, you're making me jealous. Couldn't *I* be your new boyfriend? *(He kisses her)*

EDIE Oh, Doyle, do you think you could get our picture in *Pravda?*

DOYLE Maybe, Edie.

EDIE Oh, Doyle, I simply love politics! *(They kiss passionately)*

Dissolve to Vera Venninger as she glares up at Divine's tree fort. She is dressed in copy of Divine's red fishtail gown from Pink Flamingos *and is made up to mimic Divine. Wilbur stands by, struggling with large canvas bag containing a squirming animal that we can't see. Bambi beckons them to come up to tree fort. The Venningers smile evilly and enter tree fort. Bambi points to video surveillance and hides from its camera. Vera takes stage center and goes into mean parody of Divine's glamour fits for the video camera to record.*

Cut to Divine sashaying her way back to car. A Baltimore tour bus passes by and crowd leans their heads out the

window to gawk. Divine (stuntman) suddenly startles the crowd by walking on her hands, doing cartwheels and wild tumbling acts.

Close-up of Divine's ecstatic face throughout.

Crowd on bus goes wild applauding. Suddenly we see different faces in crowd turn away from Divine in surprise. We see Divine, standing on head, suddenly distracted as she stands upright and stares in awe.

Shot of Velveeta Jones, an unbelievable 400-pound black woman in one-piece bathing suit riding down the street in sidecar of motorcycle. Her bodyguard, Puddles, a rough-looking male impersonator in blackface, slowly cruises the motorcycle through the crowded streets.

Velveeta scans the crowd like a hawk and spots a white liberal lawyer type in three-piece suit. She points to him threateningly and mouths "You!" He swallows hard, looks over his shoulder, hoping she means somebody else, and starts walking away briskly. Velveeta hops from sidecar and begins chasing him. Divine watches with the rest of the crowd in amazement. Lawyer makes mistake of trying to escape down dead-end alley. Velveeta follows and spits on hands and rubs them together. Lawyer realizes he is cornered and panics, trying to climb wall. Divine watches from end of alley as Puddles, the bodyguard, pulls gun and blocks entrance. Velveeta grabs lawyer and rips off his clothes and rapes him. Lawyer is flailing about under her massive weight. Even Divine looks shocked as she pushes her way through the crowd to Puddles.

DIVINE   Please . . . I am Divine. . . . Who is this marvelous woman? You've got to introduce me.

PUDDLES   Miss Velveeta don't take no visitors when she's out raping.

DIVINE   Nonsense *(Calling out)* Miss Velveeta! It's Divine here to see you!

Velveeta looks up and her eyes light up in respect. She gets off lawyer, who is totally stunned, gives him a big smack on the lips, and pats his head.

VELVEETA *(To Divine)*   Well, I'll be a monkey's ass! Is that really you, Divine? Let her enter, Puddles, she's my idol!

DIVINE *(Approaching her, shaking hands)*   Compliments to strangers are hardly my style, but I just have to tell you, I think you're incredible!

VELVEETA   Thank you! What an honor! I got all your clippings. In fact, every time I eat, I think of you.

DIVINE   Velveeta, you must give me your address. *(Dramatically)* I think you may be the *second* filthiest person alive. *(Velveeta cries out in delight and they embrace)*

Fade-in to Bambi, who is elaborately tied and bound in tree-fort living room.

Shot of Divine and family approaching elevator.

Interior tree fort. Bambi begins putting on phony struggling act.

Divine enters, sees her.

DIVINE   Oh, my God! Bambi! What's happened? *(Crackers II and Cotton II run to ungag her)*

BAMBI   We've been attacked! They took me by surprise and overpowered me. I fought with all my might, I swear I did!

DIVINE   Who did this?! I'll break their necks. I'll rip their larynxes out!

BAMBI   I never saw them before. A woman and a man. *(To Divine)* They were in your bedroom!

Divine's eyes widen and she rushes out.

Divine enters bedroom and surveys it suspiciously. Crackers II and Cotton II follow.

DIVINE   *Someone* has been sleeping in *my* bed! *(She approaches bed warily and rips off spread to reveal sheets stained with garbage, food)*

Cotton II and Crackers II cry out in shock.

DIVINE   The assholes gave me a pie bed! *(Remembering)* Oh, my God, my memoirs! *(Rushes to tape recorder and flicks it on. We hear Divine's voice)* ". . . Like most goddesses, I was born in humble surroundings . . ." *(Vera's voice cuts in)*

VERA'S VOICE   Yeah! A toilet bowl, my mother thought I was a turd. *(Divine screams out and fast-forwards the tape)*

DIVINE'S VOICE   ". . . to be internationally celebrated for her beauty, style, motherhood, and fashion flair."

VERA'S VOICE   And my big polkies, my BO, my bad breath, and my feminine hygiene problem. Ha ha ha ha ha ha!

DIVINE *(Trembling in rage)*   How dare this harpie hack edit my memoirs! HOW DARE SHE!!

Divine notices door to dresser rattling and she slowly approaches it and opens it. A pig dressed in a Divine-type outfit and makeup runs out squealing, wearing a sign saying "Simply Divine."

Divine screams and Crackers II and Cotton II try to catch it, but it runs into living room and they give chase. Edie and groupies scream as pig rushes in.

INEZ *(Jumping up on chair and holding up skirt)*   Oooohh, a pig!

CRACKERS II   I'll get it, Mama.

EDIE   A PORKER! *(Takes off shoe and starts banging it on table à la Khrushchev)* We will bury it! We will bury it!

DOYLE   Oh, Divine, this is an outrage!

Crackers II tackles pig.

CRACKERS II   I got it, Mama! *(Holding it up)*

DIVINE   Take that makeup off it! And burn that blasphemous dress! Who would dare mock my image like this? Irma, turn on the video. Could they be so stupid as to show their face?!

Irma turns on tape and we see Vera wildly imitating Divine into camera.

VERA How do you like that, FATSO?! Because this is just the beginning! You're old hat now! I'm the *new* filthiest person alive! This is war, PIG BREATH! TOTAL WAR!

DIVINE *(Stunned, shaking with rage)* WAR? I'LL GIVE YOU WAR, YOU SCRAWNY CHICKEN-NECKED HATCHET FACE. *(Smoke starts coming from ears)* WE'LL SEE WHO DARES CLAIM MY MANTLE, BE-STOWED ON ME BY NO LESS THAN *TIME* MAGA-ZINE, *NEWSWEEK* MAGAZINE, UPI, AP, RIGHT ON DOWN TO THE *EAST BALTIMORE GAZETTE!* *(Shaking with rage, she begins levitating off ground. Grou-pies look petrified, family looks proud)* DON'T FLING DOWN THE GAUNTLET TO ME, YOU WALKING MUD FENCE! *(Rising higher in air, to everyone's aston-ishment)* TAKE YOUR CRUSADE OF CRAP SOME-WHERE ELSE, MULE FACE! BECAUSE BY LAND, BY SEA, BY AIR, I'LL GET YOU! AND I'LL GET YOU GOOD! *(Her head spins around 360 degrees as groupies cry out in fear)* NOBODY FUCKS WITH THE HIGH PRIESTESS OF FILTH! NOBODY! BANZAI!! *(She is so furious that she levitates literally through the roof)*

Wipe shot to exterior Venninger home.

Front door creaks open and Vera peers out to see if coast is clear.

Cut to Wilbur pulling up outside in limo.

Wilbur beckons and Vera rushes out with three kidnapped children handcuffed together. Each kid is dressed in black jeans, high-top black tennis shoes, and black T-shirts (one has the word "Brat" on it, another "Junkie," and another "Filth").

They peel out.

Dissolve to limo pulling into suburban neighborhood and slowly cruising the quiet streets. Wilbur stops car and runs to random house and peers into window. Seeing nothing interesting, he runs to another house and sneakily spies in window. We see a children's birthday party in progress. Kids are surrounded by presents, dressed up, wearing party hats, and playing Pin the Tail on the Donkey. Wilbur looks excited and beckons for troops. Vera leaps from car and hurries nervous kids out.

VERA *(Opening kids' handcuffs)*   Go on! You know what to do! *(Kids hesitate)* Hurry up, or *you'll never see your parents again!*

Interior birthday party.

Kids have moved to birthday boy's table as mother brings in cake with candles and all sing "Happy Birthday."

Shot of Tracy, Jimmy, and Larry as they throw outside barbecue pit through plate-glass window and attack the party. Birthday guests panic as the terrorists smash presents and knock over furniture. Mother tries to stop kids but they leap on her, pulling her hair. Table is knocked over and Larry shoves cake into mother's face as Tracy takes the donkey tail and pins it on mother's behind. Jimmy punches birthday boy in mouth.

Exterior house.

Vera is spray-painting "FILTH" across front door. Kids rush out yelling "Filthiest People Alive," etc. Wilbur is finishing up pouring gas on lawn. He throws a match. We see F-I-L-T-H light up in flames as the limo peels out.

Slow fade-out on burning letters.

Slow fade-in to Divine's agitated face as she drives convertible down highway toward city. It is night. She pulls up to mammoth car junkyard and gets out. Divine wanders through junkyard calling out, "Velveeta! Velveeta!" Junkyard is eerily lit and she is frightened by crazed bum who pops out of car as she searches for Velveeta's home.

Cut to Puddles, Velveeta's bodyguard, outside of Velveeta's "home," which is made entirely out of large refrigerator boxes and wrecked car parts. Puddles hears weak cries of Divine in distance and jumps to attention, pulling out gun.

Cut back to Divine still searching and softly calling out. She comes to wretched old Hag cooking a motley hot dog over a trash fire.

DIVINE   Excuse me, can you tell me where I'd find Miss Velveeta Jones?

HAG *(Eyeing her suspiciously)*   Your name Divine?

DIVINE   Well, yes it is, if it's anything to you.

HAG   I thought I recognized you. You're the filth queen.

DIVINE   Well . . . yes, I am.

HAG   I've been a cult follower of yours for a long time. *(Suddenly desperate)* Tell me the truth. Are you really God?

DIVINE *(Proudly)*   In person.

HAG   Can you *prove* you're God? Show me some sort of sign?

DIVINE   I think if I concentrated, I might be able to work up some sort of minor miracle.

Divine begins staring hard. X-ray light beams come out of her eyes toward hag's hair. Suddenly, magically, Hag's hair rises and goes into elaborate beehive hairdo. Hag is amazed and falls to knees.

HAG   Miracle! Miracle! Oh, you *are* God! You want my hot dog? Here, take it! It's all yours.

DIVINE   No, keep it for yourself, my disciple.

HAG   Velveeta Jones—third row down, past the refrigerator, it's the second cardboard box on the right.

DIVINE   Thank you. *(Divine touches Hag's head in blessing before exiting as Hag wolfs down hot dog)*

Cut to Puddles, hiding with gun behind wrecked car as Divine approaches Velveeta's box house. Puddles leaps out.

PUDDLES   Hold it right there, honky.

DIVINE   Oh, it's you, Puddles. You startled me! I'm Divine, remember?

PUDDLES *(Scowling)* Yeah . . . I remember you.

DIVINE Could you announce me to Miss Velveeta?

PUDDLES *(Begrudgingly)* I'll see if she's presentable.

Interior Velveeta's. Elaborately gaudy and cheap. Velveeta is lounging in a large vat of cherry Jell-O, dressed in another bathing suit.

PUDDLES Velveeta, that Divine broad's here to see you.

VELVEETA *(Jumping up)* Divine's here!? Oh my God, show her in!

Puddles stomps outside to Divine.

PUDDLES Her nibs will see you.

DIVINE Thank you, Puddles. *(She enters)*

Interior Velveeta's. Divine rushes to Velveeta, who is still in Jello-O vat.

DIVINE Velveeta, darling. *(They kiss the air beside each other's cheek)*

VELVEETA God, girl, I didn't think you'd *really* come to visit! You mind if I stay put right here in my Jell-O?

DIVINE No . . . it looks sort of comfortable.

VELVEETA Oh, it is! I rape all day and by night I'm tired! I swear by my Jell-O. It's good for the circulation. You ought to try it sometime. *(Rolling around)* Soooooooo soothing!

DIVINE   Velveeta, nothing could soothe me tonight. I came because I need your help. Someone brazenly attacked my home today!

VELVEETA   Want me to *rape* 'em?

DIVINE   I don't even know who they are. *(Takes out photos developed from video cameras)* Have you ever seen this woman? And I use the term loosely.

VELVEETA *(Studying the photos)*   Lassie? Benji? Rin-Tin-Tin? I never saw this dog, Divine, but I've lived in this godforsaken community of Baltimore all my life. I got contacts up the ass! Rest assured, Velveeta will locate this tired bitch.

≋≋≋

Wipe shot to Vera Venninger, dressed in black, overdramatically playing the organ in Venninger Funeral Home as Ashburn mourners mill about looking anything but upset.

Shot of Ashburn corpse laid out in open coffin as Wilbur watches adoringly. Two teen-age mourners are kneeling in front of coffin.

TEEN A *(Giggling)*   You still tripping, man?

TEEN B   Yeah! Want to set off a cherry bomb in her mouth? I got one right in my pocket.

TEEN A   Nah, fuck her! Let's go steal money from the pocketbooks.

They exit. Mrs. Ashburn and another woman take their places kneeling.

MRS. ASHBURN   She looks awful, don't she?

WOMAN   How much did she leave us, I'd like to know.

MRS. ASHBURN   For her loving daughter, not a goddamn cent!

WOMAN   Well, I'm takin' her ring, then. *(Tries to rip it off corpse)*

MRS. ASHBURN   Oh no you don't! I paid for this funeral, so *I* get the ring.

WOMAN *(Fighting for ring)*   You've always been the cheap one in the family!

MRS. ASHBURN *(Fighting)*   Hands off, sister dear!

WOMAN   You already stole the Mix-Master before I could get it.

MRS. ASHBURN   Yeah? Well, I'm getting the stereo too!

WOMAN   Over my dead body! Cubby, she's trying to claim the stereo!

Other mourners rush over yelling "Oh, no, the stereo's mine," "Dibs on the TV," "I want the toaster!" Men start pushing each other, fights break out. Mrs. Ashburn and sister are grabbing jewelry off corpse, and coffin tips over and cadaver falls out. More fights break out. People start leaving, screaming "Fuck the funeral," "Let's go to her house now!" "First one there gets the TV," etc. People knock each other down to get out. Wilbur and Vera follow them to door.

Mourners rush from house, leap in cars, and cut each other off, peeling out, causing traffic jam.

VERA   What absolute scum!

We see paper boy walking down the street, delivering papers.

WILBUR *(Yelling out)*   You're late, paper boy!

VERA   AND WE JUST MIGHT REPORT YOU!

Paper boy looks at them disgustedly and hurls paper at them. They both duck to avoid being hit in head. Paper boy laughs and keeps going.

VERA   WE'LL HAVE YOU FIRED FOR THIS!

WILBUR   AND ARRESTED FOR ASSAULT!

Vera reaches down and grabs paper and opens it. We see Baltimore Sun *headline: "Kidnapped Children Go on Rampage!"*

VERA   Oh my God! WE MADE THE HEADLINES!

WILBUR   LET ME SEE! LET ME SEE!

Shot of Puddles hiding behind car, taking surveillance photos of Vera and Wilbur. We see them through camera and freeze-frames.

VERA   THIS MEANS NEW YORK PUBLICITY, WILBUR! New York means the world! Just think—we may even get coverage in the *International Herald Tribune*! ZURICH! BERLIN! LONDON! STOCKHOLM! WE'RE FINALLY FAMOUS, WILBUR!

Wipe to Divine in sensational gown, reading from prepared statement at large press conference. Many microphones are in front of her. Inez, Irma, Wiffle, and Waffle flank her, dressed in new "divinity" military uniforms. The press, both TV and print, eagerly record the event.

DIVINE   ... and so, gentlemen of the press, with a heavy heart, a clear conscience, and a certain amount of pomp, I must HEREBY DECLARE WAR! This is a call to arms! The Divinity Empire will never crumble!

Groupies shoot guns in salute.

INEZ *(Stepping forward)*   For a very brief time, General Divine will take your questions.

REPORTER A   Hans Dorman, *Bild,* West Germany. Is your defense prepared for war?

DIVINE   Our SWAT teams have been stockpiling guns all over the country. Hijacked tanks are being shipped from Camp David at this moment. We have a strong defense, Herr Dorman, and we plan to use it.

REPORTER B   Jim Donaldson, *Vogue.* Any comment on the kidnapped children?

DIVINE   My opponents obviously don't know the difference between good filth and bad filth. I will locate those children and return them to their parents, where they can decide to be filthy of their own free will!

REPORTER C   Billy Kolodner, *National Enquirer.* You are used to surprising the media, Divine. Well, today I have a surprise for *you.* Guess who's here to see you?

DIVINE Don't get *funny*, Mr. Kolodner. I'm feeling rather humor-impaired today.

REPORTER C Like it or not, Divine. Here they are, all the way from Biloxi, Mississippi—YOUR REAL PARENTS!

Chesty and Tubby step out of car. Media goes wild surrounding them.

CHESTY *(To Divine)* Shirley! Shirley Stapleton! *(Divine looks appalled, completely unnerved)* It's me, your long-lost mother!

TUBBY Shirley Stapleton, what are you doing in that ridiculous outfit? We raised you better than that!

DIVINE *(To groupies)* Get those people out of here! *(Groupies are too stunned to move)* Do you hear me!?

INEZ *(To Divine)* Is your name really Shirley?

DIVINE *(Aside)* Inez, if I ever hear you say the name Shirley in my presence again, you will be banished from my kingdom forever! Do you understand?!

Divine storms over to Chesty and Tubby.

CHESTY Oh my God, when is the last time you had a bath?

TUBBY Shirley, you are covered with germs!

DIVINE *(Threateningly)* MY NAME IS DIVINE NOW!

CHESTY We're well aware of this ridiculous clownlike image you've been promoting. But we're here to tell the TRUTH! That your real name is Shirley Stapleton and underneath all this phony-baloney filth nonsense, you're a CLEAN GIRL!

TUBBY   And we've written a book *all* about it. We've already sold the first serialization rights to *Ladies' Home Journal.*

DIVINE   Is that all you want, MONEY?

CHESTY *(Yelling to press)* She's TRYING TO PAY ME OFF!

TUBBY   Cover-up!

CHESTY   DIVIN-I-GATE!

REPORTER C   How does it feel to see your *real* parents again?!

DIVINE   My real mother is Edie. She would never try to use me for publicity like these MEDIA OPPORTUNISTS!

CHESTY   Don't believe her lies! I'm her real mother all right. I nursed her at this very bosom and *Oui* magazine is here to photograph them. *(Unbuttoning her blouse)* Nudity, per se, is something I'd never condone, but these NOZZLES OF LIFE prove that no one but me could have weaned such a beautiful child.

Press goes wild photographing Chesty's mammoth breasts as Divine looks on, appalled.

DIVINE   Gentlemen of the press, and I use the word *gentlemen* loosely—these *imposters,* lured out from under some rock by your checkbook journalism, know the truth! That by crashing my publicity they are forever damned to mere footnotes in the history of filth! HAS LOCAL COLOR GOTTEN THIS MEDIOCRE?! END OF PRESS CONFERENCE! NO MORE PHOTOS! NO MORE QUESTIONS! NO MORE ANSWERS!

Cut to shot of Edie, sitting on mat in nursery, surrounded by barbed wire that Doyle is looping around her.

DOYLE   There, Edie, all finished. You got your wish. You're finally behind the Iron Curtain.

EDIE   Good-bye Western Europe, hello Russia!

DOYLE   You're a real pinko now, Edie, a card-carrying Bolshevik.

EDIE   Hahahahahaha!

Divine enters. She is very upset.

DOYLE   Hello, Divine . . . *(Alarmed at her appearance)* Are you okay?

DIVINE *(Sobbing)*   You can't imagine the indignity I've just been put through.

EDIE   Who is it? Who's out there far away in a capitalist country!?

DOYLE *(To Divine)*   We've been playing Iron Curtain.

DIVINE   Oh Mother, it's me, Divine. I was just humiliated in front of the media. *(Breaking down sobbing)* I fear my image may have been irreparably damaged.

EDIE *(Snapping out of it, suddenly concerned)* Really, Divine? I'm sorry if you've had a trauma. *(Impatiently)* Doyle, move this stupid wire so I can comfort and hold my daughter.

DOYLE *(Winking to Divine, teaching Edie a lesson)* I'm afraid that's impossible, Edie. The free world's passports are not honored behind the Iron Curtain.

EDIE But Doyle, I'm bored being a Communist. My daughter needs me!

DOYLE Escape then, Edie.

DIVINE *(Through tears)* Have the courage to admit your mistakes, Mama.

EDIE *(Going into deep fantasy)* Mama Edie has seen the realities that lie behind the rhetoric of communism. She must defect! *(She begins crawling toward wire)* In the still of the night, in a remote corner of East Germany, she sneaks to the edge of the Berlin Wall. It's now or never. . . .

DOYLE You can make it, old girl!

DIVINE Just close your eyes and think of America!

They lift up corner of barbed wire and Edie crawls out.

EDIE At last! Freedom! Capitalism! America! Divine! *(Divine tearfully embraces her mother)*

EDIE Awwwwwww! Everything's gonna be okay, Divine.

Inez rushes in carrying walkie-talkie.

INEZ Checkpoint Bambi has reported that a certain Miss Velveeta Jones is here to see you.

DIVINE *(Pulling herself together)* She's our secret weapon, Inez. By all means show her in.

INEZ *(Talking into walkie-talkie)* Code Blue! Permit entry. Code Blue. Over and out.

Cut to Crackers II and Cotton II drilling Wiffle, Waffle, and Irma in living room. They march up and down in uniform, carrying rifles.

CRACKERS II Hup two, three, four. Hup, two, three, four.

COTTON II Parade rest!

CRACKERS II Guns right! *(They do formation)* Guns left!

COTTON II Parade march!

CRACKERS II Hup two, three, four. Get the lead out of your ass, Irma!

Inez and Divine come rushing out of nursery. Inez is listening to walkie-talkie.

DIVINE At ease, for God's sake. At ease!

Knock at door is heard. Inez rushes to answer it. Velveeta enters in ridiculous camouflage combat outfit.

VELVEETA *(Saluting Divine)* Velveeta Jones, reporting for duty.

DIVINE   At ease, Velveeta. (*Gesturing to groupies and family, who are awestruck at Velveeta*) This is my family and followers. . . . This is our top espionage ally, Miss Velveeta Jones. (*Everyone gives her power fist sign and cheers*)

VELVEETA   I've completed my first assignment. (*Takes out folder and hands Divine photo Puddles took of Wilbur and Vera*) It's them—the child stealers! Vera and Wilbur Venninger!

Everyone gathers around photo and makes derogatory comments.

VELVEETA   My surveillance team located them this morning. Their address is on the back.

DIVINE (*Turning over photo*)   Good work, Velveeta! D-Day is here. Man the torpedoes, bring on the tanks! 1300 North Charles Street, here we come! Vera and Wilbur Venninger, PREPARE TO DIE! (*Everyone breaks into Indian war cries*)

Cut to shot of Divine and Velveeta rumbling down Baltimore's Charles Street in huge army tank. They stop in front of Venninger house. Divine and Velveeta hop down and zigzag war-style to front of house, holding two branches in front of them for camouflage. Divine carries a bullhorn.

DIVINE   Vera and Wilbur Venninger, you are surrounded! Let the children come out first! Give yourselves up and no one will be hurt.

Interior shot of empty silent rooms.

Shot of kidnapped kids hearing and jumping up in happiness.

DIVINE   THIS IS DIVINE SPEAKING! LET THE CHILDREN GO UNHARMED! YOU HAVE EXACTLY ONE SECOND TO GIVE YOURSELVES UP OR I'M COMING IN THERE TO GET YOU! ONE, ONE THOUSAND. THAT'S IT! YOUR TIME IS UP, ASSHOLES!

≈≈≈

Cut to Vera and Wilbur rushing into 7-Eleven-type fast-food store. The staff is Vietnamese. Vera and Wilbur wait in line of customers.

VIETNAMESE *(In heavy accent)*   That's six dollars.

CUSTOMER A   For a loaf of bread?

VIETNAMESE   Go somewhere else if you don't like!

CUSTOMER A *(Paying)*   What a rip-off! *(Exits, shaking head in disbelief)*

CUSTOMER B   Just a half-gallon of milk, please.

VIETNAMESE   Six dollars fifty.

CUSTOMER B   You gotta be kidding!

VIETNAMESE WIFE *(Butting in)*   That's what you get for your imperialist aggression against our country.

VIETNAMESE   You taught Vietnamese how to be capitalist! NOW YOU PAY PRICE!

CUSTOMER B *(Throwing down money)* What's happening to this neighborhood? Don't I get a bag?

VIETNAMESE BAG IS A DOLLAR!

CUSTOMER B *(Snatching milk and leaving)* I'll never shop here again! *(Muttering to himself)* LOUSY CONG! *(Exits)*

Wilbur and Vera approach.

VERA Chi Long? I am Vera Venninger. This is my husband, Wilbur.

VIETNAMESE *(Bowing)* Mrs. Venninger, Mr. Venninger. We are honored to meet an enemy of America.

VIETNAMESE WIFE *(Whispering)* Your bomb is here. Our people deliver. Do you have the American greenbacks?

WILBUR Yes, we do, Ye Long! One thousand dollars. *(Hands it over)*

VERA We're so excited! We've never had the bomb before.

VIETNAMESE Bomb in back. You follow.

Dissolve to Wilbur and Vera lugging ridiculous bomb to U-Haul trailer hooked up to limousine.

Cut to Divine and Velveeta climbing up fire escape to roof. They approach chimney and Divine yells down through bullhorn.

DIVINE Oh, Vera and Wilbur. We're coming to get you!

Shot of fireplace in empty living room. We hear Divine's voice echoing down.

Cut back to roof. Divine throws down bullhorn and climbs on top of chimney. She motions for Velveeta to follow and suddenly jumps down chimney.

Shot of Velveeta's startled face.

Cut to shot of Venninger living room fireplace. We hear sounds of Divine's screams and then she lands in fireplace with a thud. She is covered in soot.

Cut back to Velveeta on top of chimney, looking nervous.

Cut to Divine yelling up chimney.

DIVINE You can make it, girl. On the count of three. One . . . Two . . .

Cut to Velveeta on roof. We can hear Divine's voice from chimney and Velveeta counts with her.

VELVEETA . . . three. *(She wedges herself down chimney and we see her vanish slowly)*

Cut back to living room. Divine is looking up chimney.

DIVINE You all right, Velveeta?

VELVEETA *(From chimney)* I'm stuck!

DIVINE Keep wedging yourself! Squeeze, girl, squeeze!

VELVEETA *(Struggling)* I'm trying! I'm trying! *(We see lots of soot falling and hear sounds of Velveeta struggling to free herself)* Aaaaarrrrrrggggghhhh!

We see Divine jump back and Velveeta lands on hearth. Divine pulls on her to get her out and finally she climbs out, covered in soot.

DIVINE   Okay, Velveeta. Put that tonnage to work!

Velveeta begins running from couch to chair to chair, sitting on each quickly. As soon as she sits, furniture splinters and collapses because of her weight. After she has taken care of living room, Divine applauds and laughs wildly.

DIVINE   Vera and Wilbur, you've got company!

They creep up steps to second floor. They enter master bedroom.

DIVINE   Where is that skinny bitch?

Velveeta sits on bed. It collapses.

DIVINE   Good work, Velveeta! *(Looking in closet)* Help me with this motley little wardrobe.

Divine goes through Vera's dresses, ripping them from hangers and tearing them to shreds.

DIVINE   Who designed these tired numbers? Look at this monstrosity, a size eight—how repulsive! *(Tears to shreds) (Suddenly stopping in horror)* Oh, my God! *(Takes out Vera's imitation red fishtail gown she wore in attack)* Look at this! The cheap knock-off of my world-famous fishtailed gown that she *dared* to wear in public. *(Inspecting it)* WITH FALSIES INSIDE! *(Velveeta and Divine destroy gown)*

VELVEETA *(Approaching makeup table)* Look! Here's all her tired-ass makeup to cover her ugly little features.

DIVINE *(Grabbing makeup)* Picture her face, Velveeta! A blank canvas just waiting to erupt into pimples! *(Breaking off lipstick, smearing eyeshadow)* Think of those beady little eyes surrounding that needle of a nose, bottomed off by that putrid chapped hole some would refer to as her mouth! *(Throws compacts, eyeliner, curlers to floor for Velveeta to stomp on)* I'm so mad I could just shit! And that's just what we're gonna do. Come on, Velveeta, we're gonna leave a grumpy in every toilet in this house!

Divine and Velveeta rush to separate powder rooms.

Cut to Tracy, Jimmy, and Larry in dungeon. They are screaming "HELP," "MOMMY, DADDY, IT'S ME, TRACY," "HELP," "POLICE!"

Cut back to Velveeta leaving powder room and hearing children's call for help.

VELVEETA Divine, I think I hear the children!

Velveeta and Divine charge to door. Children are yelling loudly.

DIVINE Hold on, my children. It's all right! Divine is here for you.

Velveeta rips off padlock with bare hands. Children rush to them and jump into their arms, covering them with kisses.

TRACY Thank you! Thank you!

FLAMINGOS FOREVER

JIMMY   Take us to our parents!

LARRY   Get me some methadone!

DIVINE *(Hugging the children)*   It's okay, they can't hurt you now.

VELVEETA   Your parents haven't forgotten you. They still love you!

DIVINE   Come, my children, Divine is going to take you home.

Divine and Velveeta lead children, who are still clutching on to them, from dungeon. As they descend stairs, Divine hears something and stops in her tracks.

Exterior Venningers'. We see garbage truck pull up and Bambi jumps out. She looks ravaged, and in a hurry.

BAMBI   Thanks for the ride, boys!

GARBAGEMAN   Yea, baby, anytime! Thanks for the action! What a gal!

Bambi runs to door and frantically rings bell.

BAMBI   Mr. Venninger! Mrs. Venninger! It's me, Bambi! Open up, PLEASE!

Venninger door is opened, but we do not see by whom.

BAMBI *(Suspicious)*   Vera? . . . Wilbur? *(She enters slowly)*

Cut to interior. Door bangs shut to reveal a very hostile Divine and Velveeta.

DIVINE   Well, well, well. I SMELL DEFECTION!

BAMBI *(Trying to back away)*   No, please . . . please!

DIVINE   Get her in a headlock, Velveeta!

Velveeta lunges at her and fights her into hold as kid-napped children cheer and yell encouragement from steps.

BAMBI   Please, Divine, don't hurt me!

DIVINE *(Approaching her)*   You rotten little snitch! That's what I get for trusting people! A spy! A regular little canary!

VELVEETA   Should I squeeze her to death?

BAMBI   Don't squash me! I beg of you! *(To Divine)* You're still the filthiest person alive!

DIVINE *(To kids)*   How about it, children, mercy or no mercy?

One by one, children give thumbs-down sign.

DIVINE   Out of the mouths of babes! You know what to do, Velveeta. Think of something cruel and unusual! *(Grabbing the children's hands)* Come on, you sweet little children, we're going home. *(To Velveeta)* Make sure you stay and give Wilbur and Vera a warm homecoming! Bambi, I'm afraid you just lost the Battle of Filth!

Velveeta drags off a struggling Bambi.

BAMBI   It's not fair! My rights! What about my rights?!

Wipe to Divine letting off Tracy at parents' house. Parents run out of house, delirious with happiness, and Tracy leaps into parents' arms.

Dissolve to Larry being reunited with parents in slow motion. They shower him with gifts.

Dissolve to Jimmy being let out as parents run across lawn and grab him by arm, yelling "WHERE HAVE YOU BEEN?!" "YOU'RE PUNISHED," "YOU'RE GONNA GET A GOOD WHIPPING FOR THIS!"

Divine looks saddened and shrugs shoulders.

Cut to Wilbur and Vera pulling up in front of their home in limo with U-Haul and bomb on back. They rush into house looking for Bambi.

VERA   Bambi? Bambi? She better hadn't be late today of all days.

They see leveled living room furniture.

WILBUR   Oh, my God!

VERA   Somebody's fat buttocks have been sitting on our furniture!

WILBUR   Our gorgeous antiques. Destroyed by cellulite.

VERA   Divine's been in this house. Can't you smell her?

WILBUR   What *is* that stench? It's coming from upstairs.

They sneak up steps, begin gagging, and approach powder room. Wilbur enters and lets out a howl.

WILBUR   Eeccccchhhhh! A payday! *(He lights match and frantically starts flushing)*

Turd magically slithers from toilet and rises in air. Wilbur and Vera are wide-eyed. Turd dive-bombs and just misses them. They run from room with turd chasing them and run into bedroom and slam door. Turd smashes against door.

Interior bedroom. Vera and Wilbur are petrified.

VERA   Wilbur, that turd was chasing us!

WILBUR   It's okay, Vera. Her turd is no match for our bomb!

VERA   But how can a turd fly, Wilbur? How can a turd be aggressive?

WILBUR   It's okay, my love.

Vera turns and sees her destroyed bedroom.

VERA   Oh my God, Wilbur! MY OUTFITS! My beautiful theatrical wardrobe! Cut to shreds. *(Seeing makeup)* And my makeup! *(Sobbing)* My heavily advertised, expensive makeup!

WILBUR   Quick! Let's go to the airport!

VERA   But Wilbur, suppose she found the children?

WILBUR *(Opening door, peering out nervously)*   I think the coast is clear . . .

VERA   Quickly! To the dungeon!

They rush out and down steps.

Shot of other bathroom. Dramatic music is heard on soundtrack.

Another turd creeps out of toilet and crawls across floor.

Wilbur and Vera rush to dungeon and discover it is empty.

VERA   Ohhhhh God! I told you we should have offed those brats!

WILBUR   The press will have a field day! She'll be a heroine, even to nonfilthy people!

Shot of turd sneaking down steps.

VERA   Wilbur, I smell something again.

WILBUR *(Sniffing)*   It's just your nerves, honey.

Turd slithers across floor so it is directly below Vera's skirt. Turd's point of view shot looking up Vera's skirt.

WILBUR   Rest assured! Today is the last day of the rest of Divine's life!

Turd zooms up Vera's skirt in attack. Eerie screeching noise comes from turd. Vera lets out a scream and fights turd from under her skirt. It whizzes in air around their heads as they panic and cover their heads. Vera and Wilbur rush down stairs with turd flying through air in hot pursuit. They are chased into kitchen, where Vera picks up a broom and tries to swat it as it hovers in air.

WILBUR   Kill it, Vera! Kill it!

VERA *(To turd)*   Come on! Come on! No turd's gonna chase me in my own home! *(She swats it and kills it)*

Wilbur rushes to Vera and embraces her. They stand next to stove with large pot on it.

WILBUR   Oh my darling, you saved us! I owe you my life.

VERA   Wilbur . . . you touched me. . . . You finally touched me.

As they embrace, Wilbur quizzically looks at pot.

WILBUR   Were . . . were you cooking earlier?

VERA   No . . . I haven't been near the stove all day. . . .

Wilbur nervously approaches stove and grabs off lid of pot. We see Bambi's head in pot, cooked. Vera and Wilbur jump back screaming in horror.

VERA   BAMBI!

WILBUR *(Getting aroused)*   She's dead now . . . she can finally be mine . . . I wonder where the rest of her body is. Oh my, this could be kind of a turn-on.

VERA   Wilbur, stop it! You embraced me a few seconds ago. You *CAN* control your perversion. This is *no* time for necrophilia!

WILBUR   Still . . . I better check the parlor . . . I mean *maybe* the rest of her is down there. I could use a quickie. . . . *(He rushes out)*

VERA *(Yelling after him)*   Our marriage really *is* in trouble, isn't it, Wilbur?

Cut to Wilbur in parlor. Everything looks in order. He tiptoes about.

WILBUR   Bambi . . . Bambi . . . your final lover is here. . . . *(He looks in hiding places, discovers nothing)* Where are you hiding? You naughty little torso. *(Looks in closet, nothing)* Just 'cause your head is upstairs doesn't mean I can't love the rest of you down here where it's more . . . private.

Suddenly parlor door slams closed with a bang. Wilbur jumps back in fright.

WILBUR   Vera? Is that you, honey? I'll be out in a minute. *(Approaching coffin)* I bet I know where you're hiding! Yes, before you rest in peace, it's time for one final roll in the hay!

Coffin lid pops open and a scantily clad Velveeta pops up into sitting position. Wilbur's hair stands on end and he screams in terror. He makes a mad dash for door but it is locked from the outside, as he frantically turns knob. Velveeta slowly and deliberately climbs from coffin and advances to Wilbur like a professional wrestler. She is grunting and smiling.

VELVEETA   Come on, Wilbur, I'm all ready for you. My pussy's jumpin' outa my drawers!

WILBUR   No . . . please . . .

VELVEETA   I'm gonna fuck you to death, baby!

WILBUR You don't understand . . . please . . . you're just not my type.

Velveeta lunges for him and tackles him, ripping off his coat and shirt. Wilbur cries out in terror.

Shot of Vera hearing Wilbur's shrieks. She runs from kitchen to parlor door and tries to open it, but it's locked.

Shot of Velveeta straddling a prone Wilbur.

WILBUR Help! Vera! Oh God, Help me!

VERA *(Panicked)* Who is it, Wilbur! Who's in there?! *(She grabs ax and begins chopping at door)*

Velveeta goes wild on top of Wilbur.

VELVEETA Come on, you skinny bastard!

WILBUR You're squashing me! I can't do it like this!

VELVEETA You better or we'll be here all night! Come on! Get it! Grip it! Get it! Grip it!

Vera axes door down and enters.

VERA *(In shock)* Get off him! That's my husband you're straddling!

WILBUR *(Weakly)* Help me, Vera. . . .

VERA *(Suddenly furious)* Wilbur, you *can* get aroused by a live woman! You've been holding out on me!

VELVEETA Come on, baby, you're almost there.

WILBUR   Vera, I have no choice. . . . *(He starts moaning ec-statically)* Vera, I love you. . . .

VERA   Don't climax, Wilbur, I'm warning you! I'll leave you for good!

WILBUR   I can't help it. . . . *(He starts moaning in orgasm)*

VELVEETA   That's it! Concentrate! Ohhhh!

VERA   No! Stop it! Wilbur! Stop it!

Velveeta and Wilbur both go into orgasm loudly.

VERA   THAT DOES IT, YOU BASTARD! *(She rushes out crying)*

WILBUR *(Clutching heart)*   Oh, God, my heart! Don't leave me, Vera! Please! *(Going into seizures)* Vera, help me! I'm having a heart attack!

Wilbur has final seizures and goes limp, tongue protruding and eyeballs bulging. Velveeta gives chase to Vera.

Shot of Vera running out front door, sobbing hysterically. Velveeta follows her close behind, but Vera leaps in car and peels out as Velveeta grabs for door handles.

Dissolve to Vera airborne, holding gun on pilot in small plane. Vera wears goggles and long Red Baron scarf and a tiara spelling out F-I-L-T-H in jewels. Bomb is visible in back of plane.

Shot of Irma, Inez, Wiffle, and Waffle in trenches around tree fort.

Shot of plane in sky above tree fort skywriting F-I-L-T-H.

Shot of Vera, laughing hysterically.

Shot of groupies seeing plane and yelling into walkie-talkie.

INEZ   AIR RAID! RED ALERT! *(Sirens are heard)* DUCK AND COVER! REPEAT, DUCK AND COVER!

Shot of Edie pledging allegiance to American flag that Doyle holds for her. They dive for cover under flag.

Shot of Crackers II and Cotton II jumping under chair and covering heads.

Shot of Divine grabbing Duane and "ducking and covering" under bed.

Shot of groupies shooting guns at planes.

Shot of Vera, struggling to lift ridiculous bomb. She heaves it over side of plane.

Shot of bomb falling from sky.

Shot of groupies ducking in trenches.

Shot of bomb hitting tree fort. Huge explosion.

Shot of Vera raising arm in victory in plane.

Shot of raging fire in tree fort. Fade-out.

≋≋≋

Slow fade-in to large funeral wreath: "RIP Divine." Organ music is heard.

Shot of Divine, outrageously laid out in ridiculously gaudy coffin. Long shot of entire funeral scene in front of burned-out tree fort. Grave is dug. Mourning tent has been set up for family. Mourners are the crème de la crème of filth society, some famous, some bizarre beyond words.

Shot of Edie with black eye and arm in sling, weeping uncontrollably as Doyle, scratched and bruised, comforts her.

Shot of Cotton II, deep in sorrow, being led through mourners' line in front of coffin. She is accompanied by Wiffle and Waffle, who are both in wheelchairs.

Shot of Crackers II, now blind, with dark glasses and white cane, being led past coffin with Duane, who is in drag and wears a hearing aid.

Shot of minicam trucks and reporters filming the entire funeral as media event.

Shot of Inez, now in neck brace, throwing herself across coffin, while Irma tries to comfort her. Shot of Velveeta arriving in elaborate funeral outfit on the arm of Puddles.

Filth mourners rush over to kneel in tribute before them.

Shot of crying kidnapped children looking healthy, being comforted by parents.

Shot of mysterious woman, moving along in mourners' line. She is overdressed and keeps face hidden by large black picture hat.

Shot of Crackers II, removing blind glasses subtly and peeking at mystery woman. We see mystery woman tilting hat up and realize that it is Vera Venninger.

Shot of Crackers II, eyes lighting up. He whispers to Duane, who hears perfectly despite hearing aid. Duane scampers up to Wiffle and Waffle and whispers. They look at Vera, hop out of wheelchairs, and run to Velveeta. Velveeta rubbernecks to get a look at Vera and nods.

Shot of Vera, who wears an expression of hatred as she nears Divine's casket. Puddles runs to Edie and Doyle and whispers. Their eyes light up in glee and both remove their fake casts.

Shot of Vera in front of casket.

Shot of Divine looking beautiful and peaceful. Vera spits in Divine's face. Suddenly, like a miracle, there is the sound of an explosion and coffin is engulfed in colored smoke. Vera jumps back in fear.

Shot of Crackers II and Cotton II smiling ecstatically. Coffin begins to spin around slowly in circle. Vera turns around to run, but Wiffle and Waffle step forward to block her exit.

Shot of newsmen dumbstruck.

Shot of kidnapped children in glee. Coffin is now spinning at great speed as sparks fly out and smoke explodes.

FLAMINGOS FOREVER

Shot of mourners in awe. Vera is absolutely horrified. Coffin gradually stops rotating and creakily rises to upright position. There is a moment of stunned silence. Divine's eyes pop open. Vera trembles in disbelief.

DIVINE   Vera Venninger, you're in a shitload of trouble!

Mourners go wild. Vera tries to run. Divine reaches out and grabs her by back of hair. Wiffle, Waffle, Inez, and Irma step forward and seize her. Vera fights for her life, kicking, biting, and spitting. Each grabs a limb and they carry her off, stretching her, to the cheers of the crowd. Crackers II, Cotton II, and Duane rush over to kiss Divine. Divine begins posing wildly with coffin for press. Vera is carried to stake as mourners gather twigs and kindling for bonfire. Vera is tied to the stake, screaming. Edie steps forward and puts gag over her mouth. Divine approaches.

DIVINE   Members of the press, I know you have deadlines, so I won't waste valuable news time. The execution is about to take place. *(To Vera)* Any last words for the press, Vera? *(Vera, gagged, struggles wildly)* Can we quote you, my dear? *(Vera struggles harder)* You heard her. No comment! Vera Venninger, you are living proof that on the eighth day, God created assholes. Assholism is something that must be eradicated from society. You are about to receive a one-way ticket to ASSHOLE HELL! *(Turning to crowd)* Where are the lovely little children?

Shot of Tracy, Jimmy, and Larry with parents. Each holds a large box of kitchen matches.

DIVINE   All ready, my innocent ones?

They nod happily and parents nudge them ahead.

DIVINE   Strike them, my children. Fear not.

They strike matches and approach Vera at stake. They turn to Divine for approval.

DIVINE   What are you waiting for? The hot dogs and marsh-mallows are all ready. PROCEED WITH THE BONFIRE!

Kids light kindling and fire quickly spreads. Vera is struggling wildly. Crowd looks on in revenge.

DIVINE   BURN WITCH BURN!

Close-up of Vera's face as flames engulf her.

Crowd begins wildly celebrating, dancing around bonfire in circle.

As Vera becomes a human torch, everyone passes out marshmallows and hot dogs and begins roasting them on sticks.

Shot of Vera's charred face melting in flame.

Shot of kids happily popping marshmallows in mouths.

Slow fade-out.

Slow fade-in to Divine, Crackers II, Cotton II, Edie, and Duane sitting on fallen tree in beautiful nature scene.

DIVINE   The time has come for flight once again, my children.

CRACKERS II   Where should we go this time, Mama? Let's go somewhere new!

COTTON II   How about the Cape Canaveral area? That's always sounded lovely to me.

EDIE   I don't care where we go as long as it's not Czechoslovakia!

DUANE   If we go to Cape Canaveral, can I become a eunuch?

COTTON II   That's a great new image for you, Duane. Once we move, I'm thinking of having my mouth removed surgically.

CRACKERS II   That's original, Cotton II. Maybe I'll have my legs amputated. Wouldn't I look cute on one of those little platforms wheeling myself down the street?

DIVINE   Then, it's settled? Cape Canaveral?

EDIE   CAPE CANAVERAL IT IS!

DIVINE   Cape Canaveral, get ready. You are about to receive into your community . . .

DUANE   THE . . .

COTTON II   FILTHIEST . . .

CRACKERS II   PEOPLE . . .

EDIE   ALIVE!

Dissolve to Divine, Edie, Crackers II, Cotton II, and Duane walking down the street in city. They carry suitcases and are dressed in traveling outfits. Suddenly a Baltimorean walks by with dog on leash. Dog keeps turning and sniffing at Divine. Divine smiles knowingly, as does rest of family.

Shot of dog yapping and panting at Divine. Divine winks sexily at dog. She pushes family away. Dog goes nuts on leash. Owner is horrified, tries to drag dog away. Divine's family is clapping hands in glee. Divine crouches down, trying to fake out the dog. Dog does the same back and barks at Divine. Finally we see a dog turd hit the ground. Divine looks excited. Magically, a poof of smoke engulfs turd and turd has suddenly grown to large size. Dog freaks out, breaks away from owner, and runs. Owner flees in panic. Another series of explosions, weird sound effects, and turd is gigantic size. Divine climbs up on turd and beckons her family to get on. They climb up on turd and suddenly turd takes off into air.

Filthy citizens run to wave good-bye as it vanishes on horizon.

Cut to Divine and family flying on turd over Baltimore, wind in their hair, happy. Flying shots should be beautiful —similar to Thief of Bagdad. *Final shot has Divine and family blowing kisses to camera as turd flies away like magic carpet over skyline.*

Credit roll.